To My Big Brother,
Jim,

I miss our adventures. I
am looking forward to a
major expedition in 1999.
Its been too long. Hope
to see you soon.

Mike
February 1999

CUSTOMS MODERNIZATION AND THE INTERNATIONAL TRADE SUPERHIGHWAY

CUSTOMS MODERNIZATION AND THE INTERNATIONAL TRADE SUPERHIGHWAY

Michael H. Lane

QUORUM BOOKS
Westport, Connecticut • London

Library of Congress Cataloging-in-Publication Data

Lane, Michael H., 1942–
    Customs modernization and the international trade superhighway /
Michael H. Lane.
        p.   cm.
    Includes bibliographical references and index.
    ISBN 1-56720-210-1 (alk. paper)
    1. Customs administration.   I. Title.
HJ6609.L35   1998
352.4′48—DC21   97–48616

British Library Cataloguing in Publication Data is available.

Library of Congress Catalog Card Number: 97–48616
ISBN: 1-56720-210-1

First published in 1998

Quorum Books, 88 Post Road West, Westport, CT 06881
An imprint of Greenwood Publishing Group, Inc.

Printed in the United States of America

The paper used in this book complies with the
Permanent Paper Standard issued by the National
Information Standards Organization (Z39.48–1984).

10 9 8 7 6 5 4 3 2 1

To the men and women
who serve their nations through customs

To their counterparts in industry

And to Bettsy

Contents

△ △ △

△ △ △

Preface

The sudden end to the Cold War created a vacuum in international affairs that left many nations and world leaders in search of a New World Order. Issues such as world hunger, the population explosion, the environment, and the gap between the rich and poor have come to vie with one another as the cause that might unify the world in the same way that the Cold War polarized it. Meanwhile, the global economy and duty-free trade promise to eclipse the Cold War as the dominant issues on the world agenda. Instead of summit conferences with world leaders and defense ministers discussing nuclear arsenals, today's international meetings are dominated by finance ministers discussing the global economy and the need to eliminate barriers to free trade.

The Japanese miracle, the success of the four Asian tigers, and the emergence of China as a major economic power are inspiring nations around the world to promote export programs and favor conditions aimed at encouraging investment. At the same time, newly industrialized countries are developing a consumer class that demands access to imported goods. Those countries in transition to a market economy are struggling with the concepts of free trade and more open borders.

This move to an integrated global economy has been supported by the establishment of the World Trade Organization (WTO) and the creation of regional trade agreements and economic cooperation such as the North American Free Trade Agreement (NAFTA) in North America, Mercosur and the Andean Pact in South America, Asia–Pacific Economic Cooperation (APEC) in Asia, the European Union (EU) in Europe, and the Economic Coalition of West African States (ECOWAS) in Africa.

In spite of significant progress in recent years and the dazzling success stories of open markets and free trade exemplified by Hong Kong and Singapore, the march toward worldwide free trade has had its stumbling blocks. Old habits die hard; protectionism dates back centuries and of course exists today. Customs administrations in many countries represent the first and last line of defense for those who would sacrifice the economic prosperity brought about by free trade for the apparent short-term gain of protecting uncompetitive industries. Explosive growth in international trade in the next few years in terms of volume and complexity will put the capabilities of all customs services to the test.

Now is the time for them to meet the challenge of working smoothly as parts of an informal international system while helping to encourage dynamic solid economic growth at home.

THE INTERNATIONAL CUSTOMS MODERNIZATION PROCESS

This book describes the International Customs Modernization Process (ICMP), a guide and integrating mechanism for nations determined to transform their customs administration into world-class organizations and for their partners in industry involved in the trade process. ICMP provides an approach for customs and industry that would lay the foundation for an efficient international system in which to do the following:

- collect all appropriate duties and taxes
- protect countries from trafficking in narcotics and other contraband
- contribute to the fight against transnational crime
- prohibit the entry of goods that jeopardize health, safety, and the environment
- facilitate legitimate trade, travel, and tourism that will encourage investment and economic prosperity
- promote a uniform and transparent system for customs processing worldwide

Contrary to myth, nations do not have to choose between a customs administration that effectively enforces laws at the border and prevents trafficking in contraband and one that facilitates legitimate trade. ICMP defines compliance with customs laws, cost of compliance, and clearance times through customs as the universal measures of customs effectiveness. Working back from these measurable goals, ICMP establishes a framework for modernization based on these elements:

- Assessing the Customs Environment
- Developing Customs Expertise
- Maintaining Customs Integrity
- Managing Processes
- Automating
- Analyzing Data
- Improving Enforcement
- Developing Industry Partnerships and Informed Compliance
- Auditing and Managing Accounts
- Measuring Compliance and Managing Risk
- Implementing ICMP

Each element of ICMP represents a chapter in this book and is a building block moving the customs administration ever closer to the goals of higher compliance, faster service, and lower costs by providing an integrating mechanism for cooperation between customs and other government agencies with the business community. Even more important, ICMP is a methodology for resolving the erroneously perceived conflict between the goals of protection of the borders and facilitation of trade. Each chapter explores an element of ICMP, defining its purpose and meaning in relation to customs goals. Examples of "Best Practices" from customs administrations around the world are used to demonstrate that customs reform and modernization is taking hold in many countries around the world—profitably for countries and for business.

PROMISE AND PERFORMANCE

As customs duty rates are dropping worldwide, the cost to industry of government processing—customs and other government agencies—is becoming an issue of greater concern to government, international organizations, and business.

The following will examine the failure or inability of customs in many nations to adopt reform and modernization and how customs can frustrate the intentions of world and national leaders by establishing and maintaining barriers to legitimate trade. The concept in modern business literature of a seamless system of international trade also gets a once-over. The "seams" or barriers to international trade are identified and we propose bold approaches to eliminating these barriers:

- acceding to and implementing the WTO international conventions on the classification and valuation of goods
- acceding to and implementing the World Customs Organization Kyoto Convention on harmonizing procedures for the processing of goods
- implementing an automated customs system in the UNEDIFACT standard to control and facilitate the processing of imported merchandise
- eliminating antiquated, archaic, and intrusive customs controls not serving legitimate customs goals

- eliminating non-tariff barriers at the border designed to prevent or inhibit the flow of legitimate goods

These practices are harmful to the nations employing them, and they can be replaced with a modernized seamless customs system in conformance with all international conventions. In many developing nations, customs is a major source of government revenues. The process outlined in ICMP is designed to ensure the collection of appropriate revenues without disrupting the flow of legitimate goods or the processes of complying importers. Modernized practices enable customs administrations to reallocate resources to target specific enforcement problems.

Four elements of the ICMP which are essential to removing seams and barriers to international trade are as follows:

- acceptance and implementation of all *international customs standards* on value, classification, origin, and procedures
- *automation* utilizing a common computer syntax, such as UNEDIFACT, which is the enabler for all other elements of ICMP
- *business process management* which will streamline customs procedures, ensure consistency with international business practices, and introduce a discipline and commitment to continuous improvement necessary for long-term success
- *audit* and *account management* which will ensure collection of revenue and compliance by the largest importers and revenue producers

These four uniform international practices are being implemented in many customs administrations around the world. Implementing these business practices, however, must be accomplished on a firm foundation of the following:

- *customs expertise* in classification, value, origin, inspection, and enforcement. Every element of ICMP is predicated upon the recognized professionalism and knowledge of customs as the national experts by the trade community.
- *integrity* of the organization and the individual customs offices. While ICMP includes elements with built-in internal controls and integrity checks, it is essential that the customs organization maintain and establish a well-earned reputation for absolute integrity. The temptations for customs corruption exceed that of any other government organization so that constant vigilance is necessary to ensure the integrity of processes and personnel.

National governments need to recognize that by investing in modernizing and reforming their customs administration there will be a short-term payoff in revenue collection and a long-term one in national prosperity. The ICMP provides the compelling case to the customs professional that customs reform and modernization can be achieved while increasing compliance and enforcement effectiveness. ICMP provides the tool to accomplish these goals.

Success in implementation will require action and engagement on the part of businesses trading internationally. Industry must engage with customs in the modernization process, increase the attention of top management to the customs process, and foster the training and professionalism of its global trade managers. A partnership between customs and industry is essential to ensure the orderly flow of $6 trillion of goods and billions of people across the world's borders.

A key ICMP focus is the transfer of technology and best practices from business and customs around the world. While outside help is recommended and sources for such assistance are referenced (e.g., the WCO, other customs administrations, consultants, etc.), it is essential that customs administrations not only become expert at the application of these skills but that they fully understand them and tailor them to the inherently unique circumstances of their own nation and organization.

ICMP is not a quick fix, but it can provide immediate remedies to specific problems. It demands a long-term commitment to change and improvement through the adoption of proven processes and techniques. ICMP establishes the framework for organizations adopting it to transform them into learning and knowledge-creating organizations to the benefit of employees, the organization, and the nations they serve.

The ICMP provides a framework for every customs administration to transform itself into a world-class organization. A world-class customs administration is a central element in every country's plan for participating in the global economy. Too frequently, the role of customs in international trade is overlooked in the larger context of trade and economic principles. However, it is at a nation's borders that the principles of international free trade are made real or are frustrated. A sophisticated high-performance customs service will not solve all of a country's economic, social, environmental, or enforcement problems, but almost every national and international issue and challenge has an aspect in which customs can make a contribution.

In an increasingly integrated global economy, ICMP recognizes the unique link between domestic and international issues, and how customs can provide that critical link. Finally, ICMP provides insight into the complex and changing relationships between customs and industry and other government agencies and how these relationships can be leveraged to the benefit of all.

In order for customs to realize its full potential and make its best contribution to a nation, national leaders must maintain the political will to support customs reform and modernization. Peru's President Alberto Fujimori is an example we look at in the context of a national leader providing the support and guidance to afford customs managers the opportunity to institute real and lasting reform and modernization.

— △ △ △

Acknowledgments

Though it is a lonely undertaking, writing a book is much more a team effort than I had ever imagined. Many organizations and individuals who contributed to my development and learning in U.S. Customs and in industry made this book possible. These include former Commissioners of U.S. Customs, Myles Ambrose, Mike Acree, and Carol Hallett, each of whom promoted my career and guided my development as a customs manager. Bob Dickerson and Al DeAngelus, my predecessors as Deputy Commissioner of Customs, mentors as well as friends, both set standards I could never match. Former Commissioner George J. Weise filled all of those roles for me in his tenure as Commissioner and is a role model as leader and customs modernization manager. Michelle Hunt, Director of the Federal Quality Institute, and her colleagues, Tina Sung and Carolyn Burstyn, were the inspiration and role models that inspired a thousand reforms of U.S. government agencies, including Customs. Dick Rosettie, Bob Mall, and Graham Cassano read entire early drafts that resulted in changes small to major. John Raven worked as hard on this book as I did, inspired major structural changes, and encouraged broadening the scope. It is not within my powers to do justice to all of John's recommendations. James W. Shaver, Secretary General of the World Customs Organization, is the prototype world customs reformer and provided invaluable suggestions for improving the book. Bob Mitchell and Robin Xenakes were my partners as Deputy Commissioner of Customs, and Bob rose from his sick bed to assist in this effort. Leo Morris, Bill Heffelfinger, and Mike Lovejoy wrote the problem-solving case studies. The U.S. Council for International Business (USCIB) and the International Chamber of Commerce provided encouragement for the effort. Bruce Wilson, Peter Robinson, and Joe Gavin from the USCIB were particularly supportive. Fermin Cuza is the role model for the global customs manager and would have been the ideal U.S. Customs Commissioner. Fermin did more than merely review, edit, and make suggestions. Sam Banks, currently acting Commissioner of U.S. Customs, provided real-life examples of implementation of many of the concepts of this book. Dennis Wakeman was patient in developing graphics and other supportive roles. Pam Moon, Gilda Wallace, and Pervenia Brown led a Washington Sandler & Travis Trade Advisory Services (STTAS) team that provided cheerful, prompt, and world-class development support. Mike Langan edited the entire text in record time with great skill and insight. Alan Sturmer and John Beck guided a naive first-time author through the process with kindness and patience. Rick Koonce provided support throughout the project. Malcolm Sparrow provided the ideas and inspiration for several chapters of the book as well as many innovations within U.S. Customs. Customs colleagues in the United States and around the world assisted and guided me throughout my career and in the writing of the book. Bob Schaffer, President of STTAS, provided encouragement and enthusiasm without which I would never have completed this work. Lee Sandler and Tom Travis provided an environment which enabled me to initiate and complete the work. Bettsy Lane read every word, reviewed each idea, and critiqued every chapter, proving to be as good and patient a listener and editor as wife and friend. Having acknowledged the sources of whatever is good in this work, I take full responsibility for all its shortcomings.

△ △ △

Introduction

Greater integration into the world economy raises the payoffs to increased competitiveness but also compounds the losses from failure to act. Increasingly, it is the more efficient policy regimes that will win out.

—World Bank,
Global Economic Prospects in the Developing World[1]

This book is written for anyone interested in improving the process of moving goods across international borders. A primary audience is the customs administration of any nation dedicated to efficient customs practices and procedures. The techniques and principles we zero in on should be of interest to all members of the international trade community and, in particular, global customs managers. Successful trade transactions are the result of a partnership among all participants in the trade community: customs, importers, suppliers, industry, customs professionals, trade facilitators, and policy makers. A fundamental understanding of customs procedures by all members of the trade community will result in more transparent, consistent, and effective processing of international trade transactions. Finally, the book should be of interest and value to academics, consultants, financial institutions, and international organizations interested in improving the international trade process or promoting international economic prosperity.

This book is intended to provide a comprehensive approach to transforming any customs administration into a world-class organization. An efficient, effective customs operation provides innumerable benefits to every segment of a country's economy. Governments can boost revenues through improved duty collections and attain their policy objectives. Industry can depend on facilitated processing of trade transactions and achieving greater profitability. Foreign suppliers recognize transparent, consistent customs procedures as key factors in determining trading partners. The result is an environment conducive to expanding trade.

Still, building a better customs organization and streamlining the system for processing goods across international borders will not automatically propel a nation to the top echelon of industrialized nations. But a slow, inept, corrupt, unreliable, or inconsistent customs regime will certainly condemn a nation to the bottom rung of the economic ladder. In an age of high-speed transportation and sophisticated communication and information technology, trade and investment can easily bypass those nations with a less than outstanding customs service. A competitive customs administration in the global economy is the price of entry to the club of industrialized, prosperous nations.

FRAMEWORK FOR REFORM

This book focuses on a framework of core components around which every customs organization should be built. While certain processes are central to any customs operation, it is a fact that each customs system is unique to a sovereign state. Size, geography, economic status, level of development, and policy objectives are all key elements in the customs organization. This book demonstrates how the circumstances unique to each country can be integrated with uniform practices conforming to international standards and conventions into a comprehensive customs operation.

The International Customs Modernization Process (ICMP) is the framework for customs reform. ICMP can be used by any customs organization regardless of its current state of development and sophistication. It is a systematic approach designed to elevate a customs service to the cutting edge.

ICMP is divided into four parts. Part I introduces the "fundamentals," three elements of ICMP that set the stage for future improvement. These are (1) assessing the customs environment, (2) developing customs expertise, and (3) understanding the importance of customs integrity. These elements are the foundation upon which every customs organization must be built.

Part II identifies three "enabling" factors of customs modernization: (1) Business Process Management and Total Quality Management, (2) automation of the customs process, and (3) analysis of customs data. These elements are called enablers because they provide customs administrations with new powers, capabilities, and previously unavailable possibilities. These processes open the door for customs to achieve unprecedented effectiveness.

Part III addresses advanced processes, the new capabilities made possible by and derived from the enablers identified in Part II. These include elements on enforcement, audit, industry partnership, and risk management. Part IV addresses implementation and integration of all elements of ICMP and future challenges.

ICMP can be illustrated in the following way:

As noted, ICMP was developed with the understanding that the strengths, weaknesses, and objectives of customs are not uniform the world over. The starting point and progression for ICMP can be tailored to the unique requirements of each organization. If a customs organization has an identified area of weakness or concern, ICMP can be utilized as an immediate guide for addressing that problem. If customs bears the responsibility for achieving a government policy objective, such as increasing revenue, interdicting contraband, or enforcing intellectual property rights, elements of ICMP can be implemented to meet those objectives. Over time, however, each element of ICMP should be implemented to focus attention on every aspect of the improvement process.

The elements of ICMP are interrelated and build upon each other. They may be implemented sequentially or in tandem to address problems or take advantage of opportunities. Linkages among elements must be developed over time and will be an ongoing process. When each element of ICMP has been implemented, the complete customs process will ensure that all transactions are in compliance with customs laws and that the cost of customs compliance for the government and industry is minimized. The result is a clear-cut improvement in cost, quality, and speed.

Implementing of a customs reform and modernization plan based on ICMP is obviously a significant commitment. The process is ongoing and eventually will impact every aspect of customs operations. While the changes brought about by customs reform efforts may be dramatic, customs is an ongoing operation and cannot shut down to initiate a period of reform, modernization, or reinvention. The import process and world trade must go on and proceed at an ever larger volume and faster pace. ICMP facilitates the continuation of vital customs functions while the modernization process is being put into action. The international trade process will serve as a powerful driver for national and international economic performance.

PURPOSE OF CUSTOMS

Customs organizations throughout the world hold a unique position within a country's government and within the international community. Protection of a nation's borders, collection of duties and taxes, and the operation of a customs administration are uniquely sovereign responsibilities. These domestic priorities are the core of customs operations. But customs organizations also have a special opportunity to service the international community. Customs is often the first contact foreign businesses and travelers have with the government. A satisfactory encounter with customs can encourage continued commercial activities. Customs organizations can also take part in international efforts to address common problems, including transborder criminal activities such as smuggling, terrorism, intellectual property rights violations, fraud, and money laundering. A modern efficient customs operation can contribute to domestic priorities, facilitate trade, and address complex international issues.

Customs organizations are also unique in that customs requires expertise in a broad range of subject areas. While customs business is not "rocket science," it might incorporate elements of rocket science to process an importation of rockets. Customs requires common sense and the ability to deal with complicated issues of international law, science, finance, and intellectual property rights.

Given the key role customs plays in achieving national objectives, the diversity and complexity of the issues confronting customs, and the importance of facilitating trade, the demands on customs organizations are great. Importers, brokers, travelers, carriers, the public, and political leaders all have strong beliefs about customs derived from their own vantage point as a user or stakeholder in customs performance. There may be pressure for increased revenue, faster service, more reliable information, better statistics, increased protection of environmental and agriculture controls, and improved enforcement performance, simultaneously from a range of different constituents. At the same time that trade, travel, and tourism are increasing and placing additional pressure on the customs organization, budgets and staffing may be holding steady or even being cut.

These demands, pressures, and apparently conflicting requirements can create stress and chaos in the organization and a sense of futility on the part of managers and employees. There is a need to create order and simplicity out of the chaos and complexity of the environment. ICMP gives the organization and manager the tools necessary to take control of the environment. The first elements of ICMP, the fundamentals (assessing the environment, developing customs expertise, and improving integrity), should prove invaluable in that regard. But we need to begin by examining the purpose of customs, and reconciling apparently conflicting and difficult demands placed upon customs.

Many factors can converge to make customs one of the most difficult jobs in government. These factors include tensions caused by the following:

- increased workload and static budgets
- demands for better facilitation and increased enforcement
- conflict between domestic industry and importers
- more passengers and freight and limited facilities for customs processing
- peaking in airlines flights resulting in thousands of airline passengers arriving at nearly the same time

Up until recent years, there was not a real way to resolve these apparent conflicts. Customs managers felt forced to choose between facilitation of trade and passengers on the one hand and strict enforcement of laws on the other. In fact, the best thing that could be done until now was to cope. But now there is a process, ICMP, which includes three technologically advanced and mature tools with which we can achieve these various goals and expectations. These tools are Business Process Management (BPM) and Total Quality Management (TQM), information technology (automation), and advanced analytical techniques. These management tools enable managers to approach their work in new ways and enable organizations to attack problems that could not have been envisioned in the past with the tools then available.

In its most simple terms, the goal of customs is to increase compliance with the laws of a nation at its borders. Those laws may have to do with revenue; classification of goods; preventing the entry of contraband; collecting fees and taxes; and enforcing agricultural, health, safety, and environmental laws. In each case, the goal of customs is to increase compliance, moving ever closer to 100-percent compliance. ICMP provides the framework for achieving that goal with the most sophisticated techniques, systems, and tools. A particularly important element of ICMP in this regard is measuring compliance, which tells us where we are in our quest to better it.

Another important goal of customs relates to the cost of achieving compliance. Industry, carriers, importers, and exporters make decisions on trade and investment in economic terms. If a customs administration is creating barriers in terms of costs, time, unreliability, and uncertainty, traders and investors will take their business elsewhere. At the same time, the customs service itself is concerned about costs since few countries have sufficient resources to permit customs to inspect every shipment and conveyance and scrutinize each customs transaction.

ICMP will enable the customs administration to achieve higher levels of compliance while lowering the cost of compliance to industry and customs. The goal of customs can be conceptualized in two parts: first, to increasing compliance to draw ever closer to 100-percent compliance, and second, reducing the cost of compliance.

Customs goals can also be illustrated in graphic terms. In Figure I.1, the goals of customs are illustrated by hitting the target of high compliance and low costs simultaneously. Point A on the Compliance/Cost chart symbolizes an impoverished customs service—one that serves its nation poorly, at low cost but with low compliance. Point B represents an ineffective, inept, or corrupt customs administration or one that is having difficulty coping with change and growth in world trade—one that fails to protect revenue or enforce laws, but is costly to the trade community. This customs administration will jeopardize the prosperity of its nation by driving away business and investment. Point C is representative of an antiquated customs administration. High compliance is achieved at high cost. This means that the customs organization has failed to modernize and is using outdated customs procedures, inspecting nearly 100 percent of shipments, scrutinizing all entries both large and small, failing to apply risk management techniques, and not capitalizing on automation and other tools of the modern customs organization. Again, the high cost to industry may discourage business and investment. The high cost to government drains scarce resources which could be employed for other purposes.

The target in Figure I.1 represents the goal of every customs organization. High compliance is achieved at the minimum cost to both government and industry. ICMP is the methodology that places that goal within the reach of every customs organization.

ICMP also provides a capacity for measuring the status and improvement of a customs agency. There is an old adage that says, "That which is measured improves." Measurement is also a tool to motivate employees. It has been demonstrated that workers are motivated when they believe they are making measurable progress toward important objectives. ICMP provides a framework for measuring progress toward the world-class customs goal.

GETTING STARTED

Fundamental modernization and reform of an organization as vital as customs demands the absolute commitment to the effort at the very highest lev-

Figure I.1
The Target: Win–Win

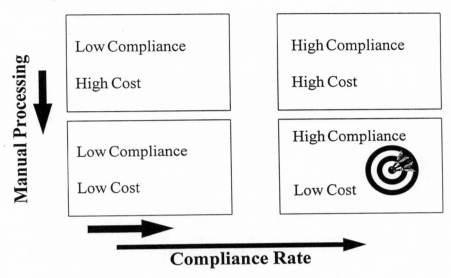

els of government. The government, top officials, and other customs administrations must provide the political will to make customs reform a reality. Without support from the government within which customs operates, the prospects for comprehensive reform are discouraging. The government, top officials, and the customs administration must provide the political will to make customs reform work. ICMP is a long-term, continual process. Support for the initiative must be maintained for implementation to be successful.

All levels of the customs organization itself must be apprised of the purpose of the modernization effort, its effects on each aspect of customs operations, and the role customs employees play in the process. Change to the organization can be traumatic, and a failure to clearly communicate the goals and process may result in the undermining of the reform effort from within.

Finally, the trade community should be a participant in the reform initiative. By demonstrating to it the cost benefits to be realized, industry would have a stake in furthering modernization efforts. Industry must be aware of its responsibilities in the trade transaction to achieve the goal of high compliance. Business input in the process can result in procedures which satisfy government requirements with the least burden on industry itself. Success in improving the customs process internationally will require top management in business to give greater attention and support to the customs function through such actions as the establishment of the position of Global Customs Manager.

Ultimately, the responsibility for bringing these many interests together into an efficient process rests with the customs organization and the government. There are sources and organizations, however, which assist in the modernization of customs operations. Use of such resources can supplement in-house knowledge, provide special expertise, broaden perspectives, or address specific issues. The following is a short list of such resources, beginning with the most important source of expertise and support for customs modernization efforts.

- The World Customs Organization (WCO) should be the initial source for support in any customs modernization initiative or customs problem. The WCO is staffed with experts from around the world knowledgeable in every customs discipline. Customs organizations which are not currently members should join. Members should avail themselves of services and support, which include a Customs Reform and Modernization Program.

- The International Chamber of Commerce (ICC) has a Memorandum of Understanding with the WCO and has developed Customs Guidelines. The ICC Guidelines mirror the goals of the WCO and suggest a partnership between customs and industry to work toward mutual goals. A copy of the ICC Guidelines is in Appendix A.

- United Nations organizations, notably the United Nations Conference on Trade and Development (UNCTAD), provide assistance for customs purposes. UNCTAD provides specific support for customs automation (see the Columbus Declaration, a set of detailed recommendations for action by customs administration, which was presented by the WCO Secretary General at the UNCTAD Trade Efficiency Seminar, in Appendix B).

- The World Bank, the Inter-American Development Bank, the Asian Development Bank, and other international financial organizations may provide support to customs organizations determined to modernize and reform. The WCO is working with the World Bank to include customs modernization in loans to developing nations.

- Business can often provide support in applying advanced business techniques, such as benchmarking, best practices, and business process improvement, to the customs process. Business can also provide insights into trade practices to be considered when developing customs processes.

- Data-processing firms can be the source of expertise in the development of systems and automation, which are the foundation for basic and advanced customs systems.

- Audit and accounting firms can be an important resource and source of expertise in supporting and performing audit functions. Audits are the basis for collecting and protecting revenue and ensuring compliance of major importers.

- Consulting firms can provide expertise in various areas throughout the process to supplement in-house skills.

- Specialized firms and universities can be employed for skills in risk management and statistics that are fundamental to process improvement but are not ordinarily available in-house.

- Other customs services are frequently the best source of expertise and experience, and are quite willing to help in the improvement process. Coordination with other customs services can also further seamless processing of trade transactions.

• Firms specializing in process and quality improvement can be instrumental in establishing, developing, and maintaining a long-term program for customs modernization.

A prudent customs organization uses as many resources as appropriate for support and expertise. But while outside perspective and expertise are critical, *customs must maintain control of the modernization process.* Vision, mission, and direction are the domain of customs officials and must support customs and government objectives. Dependence on outside organizations can hold the customs organization captive to their expertise and reduce flexibility to address unique circumstances if the customs administration fails to take ownership of the modernization effort. The objective of each use of outside help should be not only the substantive task but also the transfer of the technology, knowledge, and expertise to the customs administration.

PRESHIPMENT INSPECTION

It is important to comment on one option currently employed by some customs administrations: Preshipment Inspection (PSI) services. Many countries have employed or are considering employing PSI companies to address deficiencies in their customs operations, revenue collection activities, or integrity. While there may be some immediate advantages to the use of PSI services, there are also a number of significant disadvantages, which may include high costs, long-term dependency, and implementation of outdated customs methodologies. There is little or no incentive or capacity for these companies to transfer state-of-the-art customs practices to the customs administration. Customs is the sovereign responsibility of government. The WCO and ICMP now provide the tools of modernization and reform for all countries to retain control of their borders and customs function.[2]

NOTES

If you are interested in obtaining more information on customs modernization or would like to provide information, examples, or case studies, or, if you would like to obtain a copy of the *Handbook on Customs Modernization*, an abridged version of the book in booklet form, please contact the author:

> 6723 N. 25th Street
> Arlington, Va. 22213
> Telephone: (703) 534–1369
> Fax: (703) 534–7160

1. World Bank, *Global Economic Prospects in the Developing World* (Washington, D.C.: World Bank Discussion Papers, 1995), 4.

2. For a detailed treatment of PSI companies, see Patrick Low, *Preshipment Inspection Services* (Washington, D.C.: World Bank Discussion Papers, 1995).

PART I

THE FUNDAMENTALS

CHAPTER 1

The Environmental Assessment

> *Though the encouragement of exportation, and the discourage-*
> *ment of importation are the two great engines by which the mer-*
> *cantile system proposes to enrich every country, yet with regard to*
> *some particular commodities, it seems to follow an opposite plan*
> *to discourage exports and encourage imports.*
> —Adam Smith, *The Wealth of Nations*[1]

One of the great challenges facing contemporary organizations and their leaders is dealing with uncertainty and ambiguity. Dealing with an unknown future is a problem that has challenged organizations for centuries, but the pace of change in the modern world is unprecedented. Scientific and technological advances are changing the way we work, live, communicate, and travel. In the world of work, improvements in information technology double the amount of information available for decision makers every seven years. These new capabilities and the quickening pace of change are a challenge for all organizations and managers. For customs, the problem is compounded by workloads that double every five or ten years, work that is made more complex by new trade agreements, and the variety of goods to be classified and appraised that includes all products under the sun arriving from the four corners of the world. Determining the direction of the organization, developing strategies to achieve organizational goals, and making the best decisions for today as well as the long term is a daunting task that can result in "future shock." Making matters worse are daily pressures to respond to the immediate needs of the environment and the current and ongoing workload. Succumbing to the temptation to focus on today's issues in the hope that tomorrow will take care of itself is a formula for disaster. Ignoring the daily business to focus entirely on the future can result in a chaos that prompts the removal of all top management.

It is a fact of life as we approach the twenty-first century that customs must cope with immediate and pressing problems in a way that satisfies multiple constituencies today and plan for a future that provides substantially improved results in terms of service and compliance. While most of us may not be visionaries, we can develop a vision of customs for the future by a systematic assessment of where we are, a look at general trends in the world at large, and a view of specific trends in areas related to customs. This chapter contains (1) an assessment of the customs environment, (2) a look at customs and the world, (3) examples of emerging trends that might impact customs, and (4) a review of new technology and business trends that may impact customs. While these actions will not yield a vision in the classical sense, they represent practical and prudent steps for a customs service concerned with preparing itself for the future.

ASSESSING THE CUSTOMS ENVIRONMENT

Our environmental assessment begins with a look at the customs world and an honest and critical assessment of customs performance and operations. In this sense, customs is fortunate in that the World Customs Organization in Brussels, Belgium, creates and administers international standards and procedures and provides support and guidance to customs in meeting their obligations under those standards.

A defining characteristic of a world-class customs administration is conforming with all international customs conventions, practices, and procedures. The WCO can be of great value and support to a customs administration beginning the journey toward self-improvement. A world-class customs organization must be in harmony with world conventions relating to customs, must have a statutory framework for enforcing customs laws, and must have the customs expertise to enforce those laws and carry out the customs mission. The following checklist is provided as a guide to assessing a country's standing among the world's customs administrations:

- Have you implemented the Harmonized System Convention?
- Have you acceded to the WTO Valuation Agreement?
- Have you acceded to the Kyoto Convention on the Simplification and Harmonization of Customs Procedures and the Nairobi Convention on Customs Enforcement?
- Have you automated customs processes utilizing a worldwide standard such as UNEDIFACT?
- Did your automation program merely automate existing manual processes, or did it truly redesign those processes to take advantage of full benefits of the automated tools and simplified processing?
- Have you requested support from the WCO in the form of the Customs Reform and Modernization Program or conducted a diagnostic study to assess your needs?
- Have you reviewed the Columbus and Arusha Declarations and made efforts to implement them, including the elements pertaining to integrity and training?
- Have you reviewed and implemented the customs guidelines promulgated by the International Chamber of Commerce?
- Have you instituted training programs for employees that have resulted in real expertise in fundamental customs disciplines of classification, value, origin, and inspection?
- Have you developed training programs or competencies in more advanced customs-related disciplines, such as audit, risk management, compliance measurement, and automation?
- Does customs have the appropriate powers under national laws to implement international customs conventions?
- Does customs have the authority to achieve its enforcement and compliance goals (i.e., arrest, seizure, and detention powers)?
- Does customs have a training academy and the capacity to train its personnel and develop expertise in every area of customs?
- Are the customs mission, goals, and strategy published and communicated to all personnel and the public?
- Does customs have mechanisms for communicating with the international trade community, publishing rulings, and allowing for appeals of decisions?

• Does customs have a code of conduct for employees that emphasizes the responsibility of employees in positions of trust?

The questions raised and the issues identified should be examined and studied closely. Accession to the conventions and development of the skills and disciplines outlined here are fundamental to the operation of a professional customs organization. Even more important is that action be taken to *implement* the substance of the international conventions and to practice and implement the fundamental skills of the customs profession. In order to implement the customs, administration must have the necessary laws and authorities. As customs mission and goals are derived from international and national laws and conventions, so it is appropriate that we initiate our process with a review of these laws. Plans and strategies for implementation must be developed. The WCO, other customs administrations, consulting firms, and private industry are available to provide assistance in training and implementation. While it is essential that customs gets its own house in order, it is equally important that customs not focus so much on internal issues that it neglects the world around it and the vital role of customs in international trade. In the following section, we address the critical issue of change and the future in an increasingly global economy.

CUSTOMS AND THE WORLD

Because no organization operates in a vacuum, the ICMP environmental scan includes an assessment of the world in which customs operates. Assessing this external atmosphere, predicting the impact it will have on customs, and developing plans for meeting the challenges of the future is the responsibility of the leaders and top management of an organization. All organizations are positioned in hierarchy, have multiple constituencies, serve many masters, face challenges by competitors, and compete for resources and budget.

Customs is unique among government organizations in that it is neither wholly a domestic or international agency, but an agency positioned on a country's international borders looking both inward and outward. Customs serves all organizations of government with border interests, including health, safety, enforcement, agriculture, and environmental agencies, and therefore must be alert to priorities in these areas for these agencies. This unique positioning requires that the customs organizations have a clear understanding of national domestic politics and the nation's position in the world economy. Customs position at the borders provides an opportunity and perspective for spotting trends in world events, trade, and transnational crime before most other agencies of government do.

Misreading events or failing to perform the customs environmental assessment can do major damage to the customs organization and to the nation it serves. The external environmental assessment is an ongoing responsibility of leadership and, while of paramount importance, is not as difficult to perform as might first be imagined. The first step in the external environmental assessment is to keep apprised of major events around the world. This is accomplished, in part, by doing the following:

- reading the major newspapers and monitoring other news media with an eye toward news that might impact customs or areas where customs might have an impact
- subscribing to the major business, trade, and international journals and magazines to identify issues of significance to customs
- joining the World Customs Organization and participating in its activities
- monitoring the activities of the World Trade Organization and other international trade organizations
- monitoring the activities of U.N. and international organizations on trade, labor, environment, health, safety, and narcotics
- participating in seminars on trade sponsored by international, government, and business organizations
- monitoring the speeches of national policy makers in the executive and legislative branches and business community
- tracking improvements in business process management and data-processing technology that may apply to customs
- tapping the Internet for general and specific information of possible value to customs
- developing relationships with business organizations representing the trade community, including carriers, brokers, importers, and exporters

The objective of each of these activities is to understand the world in which customs operates and the opportunities and challenges that customs may face in the near or long term. With its unique perspective at the international borders, customs has the opportunity to view and identify events and trends in the domestic and international arenas. The goal is not to react to events, but to anticipate the future to the benefit of the agency, the sovereign state, and the international trade community. Customs is the bridge from the international to the domestic, and of course back again from the domestic to the international. Sensitivity to events and trends in both worlds is therefore a necessity. This unique position also affords customs the opportunity to increase understanding between the domestic and international domains.

Information and knowledge obtained through the actions outlined will be strategic in nature. It may be used to set or challenge the direction of the organization, however, it will ordinarily be of greatest value when used in conjunction with other information gathered in the environmental assessment process in order to give a comprehensive picture of customs and the world in which it operates.

EXAMPLES OF EMERGING TRENDS AND
CHANGES IN ENVIRONMENT

As discussed, the environmental assessment, using both formal and informal approaches, is an ongoing responsibility of customs leadership. Failure to identify emerging trends and major events can have an adverse impact on customs operations. These examples of emerging trends over the past several decades have substantially impacted customs operations:

- the advent of container ships and containerized cargo, which demanded new port facilities and disrupted traditional cargo inspection techniques
- the increase in air freight, which demands faster clearance and cargo inspection facilities at airports
- the movement to intermodal transportation systems, which mandated seamless transfers between modes of transit and borders
- the emergence of the air courier industry, with increasing demands for rapid-release times, off-hours, and new locations
- the increased emphasis on accurate trade statistics and their importance in measuring economic performance
- the new international emphasis on Intellectual Property Rights (IPR) that predated IPR legislation in some countries
- the introduction of regional trade agreements that reduced tariffs and other trade barriers and procedures carried out by customs
- the creation of the WTO to strengthen the worldwide trade reforms of the GATT in areas such as classification, value, origin, and customs procedures

Customs administrations which used the techniques of environmental scanning and assessment were able to participate in the development or shaping of these initiatives. At a minimum, they were aware of the emergence of these issues and were able to develop plans and strategies to deal with the impact on customs operations. Customs administrations which failed to apply the techniques of environmental assessment and scanning more than likely encountered difficulties in the following areas:

- decreased effectiveness in customs enforcement and compliance
- delays in processing, additional costs, and backlogs of entries
- loss of attractiveness as an international business center, with a consequent loss of trade and investment
- loss of public confidence in the ability of customs to provide services and effectively enforce laws

In addition to events and trends international in scope, customs and its leadership must be attuned to national trends and goals. New economic and trade plans, trends toward free trade or protectionism, efforts to downsize government or reduce government spending, plans to expand trade or open new airports or seaports, and concerns about the environment, drug abuse, and contraband are all examples of issues that may impact customs or on which customs may have an impact. In the global economy, domestic criminal organizations seize on new opportunities to link with international criminal organizations, often resulting in international money laundering, narcotics trafficking, and other international crime cartels. Customs may be the first agency to discover these emerging crime problems—and can be the first to act on them. Failure to act on these problems early on enables the criminal organization to establish a stronghold that may be difficult to break. The rise of international trade as the primary issue of our time has become coupled with the emergence of transnational crime as the number-one crime problem. Individual customs administrations and the entire international customs community could be a major deterrent and force against transnational crime, provided that customs administrations take the leadership to unite against it.

The government of Poland is an example of a customs administration in transition to a market economy after forty years of state monopoly and restriction of foreign trade. Poland had to build a customs system essentially from the ground up. The opening of the Polish economy was accompanied by dramatic growth in travel and trade, and new problems with enforcement and compliance. Poland determined it was necessary to integrate its customs system with those of Western Europe and to achieve conformity with WTO principles as well as WCO conventions. The story of Poland's customs reform and modernization began with an in-depth, honest, and objective assessment of its environment, which was used as a basis to initiate the transformation (see Appendix C for more detailed information on the reform of Polish Customs).

ASSESSING NEW TECHNOLOGICAL DEVELOPMENTS AND BUSINESS TECHNIQUES

New developments in technology and new techniques in business are other areas that customs leaders must monitor. Examples in this area include the following:

- improvements in transportation technology by ground, sea, and air
- changes in logistical and supply systems, such as just-in-time inventory
- breakthroughs in technology in communications or information processing
- new business approaches such as Total Quality Management and Business Process Management
- developments in statistics, measurement, and risk management
- scientific advances in chemistry and biology
- emerging processes, such as artificial intelligence and computer modeling

Each of these categories of change represents opportunities for the alert customs organization to improve its efficiency and effectiveness. It may be a truism to state that many new trends or emerging technologies turn out to be fads, flops, frauds, or worse. Some organizations run from one new management fad to the next with no focus or purpose, creating cynicism within the workforce. Others may experiment or dabble with the right tool and fail in implementation. None of these management tools in themselves can transform the organization. However, when properly selected and applied, new technologies and management approaches can and do have a role in helping the prudent customs organization achieve its long-range goals. What is vital is that the leadership of the organization review each of these tools in a critical fashion and evaluate them in terms of how they fit into the context of the strategic plans of the organization, how the new approach would be introduced and implemented into the organization, and what other changes in structure should accompany the innovation. Without such deep thinking and planning and inclusion of employees and stakeholders, even good techniques are doomed to fail.

APPLYING THE INFORMATION AND KNOWLEDGE GAINED THROUGH THE ENVIRONMENTAL ASSESSMENT

There is no beginning or end to customs environmental assessment. It is an ongoing process of collection of strategic information that may be of value to the organization in its strategic and long-term planning. Some organizations have a formal strategic plan, a planning process, and planning organization. If so, the information gathered can be provided to the planning group to factor into the strategic planning process. Other organizations have less formal or ad hoc planning approaches. In any case, information is collected with an organizational intent to use it where appropriate. Information must be analyzed to separate the true from the false, the important from the trivial, and the relevant from the irrelevant.

For this analysis, the following questions should be asked:

- Is this information relevant to our organization? If so, how? Why?
- What is the source of this information and how will this information impact us?
- Is this information accurate? How can it be verified?
- Can we use it to eliminate red tape or outdated procedures?
- How can we take advantage of this information?
- Is this a one-time occurrence?
- How can we learn more about this event or issue?
- How does this information or event fit in with our ongoing operations?
- Is the information time sensitive? Must we move quickly?

As these questions are being asked and the information is being analyzed, the organization must consider what steps should be taken to capitalize on it and the impact and cost of acting or not acting. Questions that may be asked in this regard include the following:

- How do we take advantage of this opportunity?
- Does this event require legislation?
- How do we protect ourselves from this problem or threat and perhaps turn it into an opportunity?
- What new skills or competencies do we need to capitalize on this opportunity?
- Does this action require a change in our organizational structure?
- Can we afford to act on this?
- Can we afford not to? What are the costs of acting versus not acting?
- What are the long-term consequences to the nation, the organization, and the employees of acting or not acting on this information?

The environmental assessment must be an ongoing process in which top management and employees are alert to external events that may pose challenges or opportunities for the organization. The process may be formal or informal, but the information captured should be used in structuring the organization's strategic plans.

CONCLUSION

Gathering strategic information through the customs environmental assessment is a fundamental responsibility of top management. The application of this information and knowledge is crucial to the survival and success of the organization and the ability of the customs administration to serve the nation, and should be a major focus of the organization's leadership. The collection and assessment of information pertaining to (1) specific changes in the customs environment, such as new international trade conventions; (2) events in trade and transportation having an impact on customs; and (3) advances in business, science, and technology ensure that customs is forewarned of challenges and opportunities in its areas of responsibility. Collecting and assessing this information carries with it the responsibility for acting on the information by developing plans and implementing programs to meet the challenges and opportunities identified. In some cases, this may be best accomplished by using the information and knowledge to alter the mission and vision statement, and to establish the direction of the organization through the strategic planning process. In most cases, the mission, structure, and goals will not be changed and the information will be acted upon with existing mechanisms or the establishment of task forces or temporary teams. The information gained in the environmental assessment is also used to enlighten and inform every other element of ICMP.

Recommendations from Chapter 1

- Perform a self-assessment of your nation's implementation of the world's customs conventions.
- Institutionalize a process for monitoring national and world events that may impact customs or that customs might impact.
- Monitor events and technology related to trade, travel, and transportation.
- Monitor national and international crime problems and trends in search of criminal activities which might have a border nexus.
- Monitor trends and techniques in business processes and technology that might apply to improving customs practices and processes.
- Develop a capacity for reviewing, analyzing, collating, comparing, and integrating information from these various sources.
- Disseminate all relevant findings from the environmental assessment to all major offices and officers of the organization.
- Develop relationships with universities and other research institutions to keep abreast of trends, patterns, and events in the political, economic, and world trading arenas.

Actions for Global Customs Managers for Chapter 1

Customs plays a key role in international trade. Every international trade transaction involves at least two customs interventions, one at export and one at import. It is clear, therefore, that the manner in which customs conducts its business has a substantial impact on the movement of goods across international borders.

—Columbus Declaration

Figure 1.1 represents some of the organizations involved in the international trade process. One could add to the chart these additional participants in the process: importers, exporters, brokers, port authorities, international and domestic carriers, bankers, attorneys, and warehousemen, among others. Though customs is "uniquely positioned" to coordinate these activities into a seamless process, it is a Herculean task. Too often, however understandably, customs officials narrowly define the scope of their responsibilities to the strictest domain of customs. Some customs administrations operate as if there were no linkage to other agencies which operate on the border or in the ports. Effective customs administration must take into account all government requirements to clear goods or passengers. Customs must take the lead in providing a point of contact for the public on border control and entry issues.

Figure 1.1
Customs and Other Government Agencies

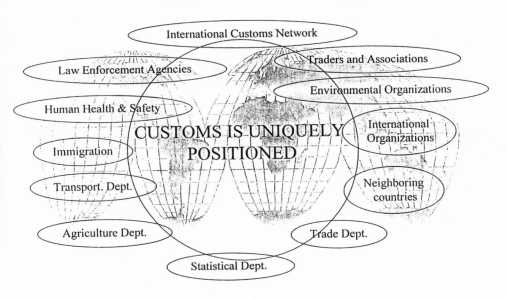

This same logic can be applied to airport passenger clearing. Customs' natural inclination is to measure the time required for its own processing, which is usually a matter of minutes; forget the hour or more required for immigration, agriculture, or facilities problems. But the importer or passenger does not make so fine a distinction. In their view there should be a process from end to end for passengers and cargo moving across international borders; indeed a seamless process. In Chapter 4, we will discuss Business Process Management techniques and the need to align the processes of the many organizations involved in the trade and travel processes. It is clear that the delays in these processes are caused by the "hand-offs" among processes and the failure to align processes or see the process as a whole. The WCO and the ICC seem to be converging on the idea that customs might be the logical organization to bring these processes together. If that is to be the case, it will require these other organizations in government and industry to cooperate with customs to develop the seamless international process. Many customs officials and some industry members see import and export as two distinct processes and fail to see the benefits to all parties of viewing export and import as an integrated transaction.

A first step in this direction must be for industry to get itself organized to a degree similar to customs at the international, regional, and national levels. At the international level, customs has the WCO, a first-rate international and coordinating body. At the regional level, customs has organizations such as APEC, which has taken leadership for customs function in the Asia–Pacific area. Of course, every country has a well-established customs administration. While businesses are well positioned individually to optimize their global affairs, the response of the business community as a group has been fragmented. Business must organize to address the international trade process at three levels: international, regional, and national. Three words of advice to global trade managers: engage, engage, engage. The ICC provides the appropriate platform for the business community to engage with customs and international organizations to improve the customs process internationally, regionally, and nationally. Customs and other international organizations have opened the door to cooperation with the business community. Many individual companies and some trade associations are taking advantage of this unprecedented opportunity of customs openness.

The recommended approach is for business to conduct its own environmental assessment. In conducting the business environmental assessment, the following actions are suggested:

- Review the questions posed earlier in this chapter from your perspective.
- Engage with customs in the environmental assessment process and provide information from the perspective of your organization.
- Assess the degree that your organization, company, industry, or association has engaged with customs at the national, regional, and international levels.
- Develop plans and a mechanism for more active participation with customs at all levels, using platforms such as the WCO/ICC MOU (memorandum of understanding) and Customs Guidelines.
- Develop a partnership approach for dealing with customs recognizing their enforcement and compliance responsibilities as well as their facilitation roles.

Business is understandably willing to invest when returns accrue to the individual company, and reluctant to spend when the returns accrue to all—even when those returns are higher. Too often the industry chair at the table has been vacant. More than at any previous time, the customs door is wide open to industry participation and partnership at the international, regional, and national levels. The time is right for customs and its partners to seize the opportunity to cooperate to improve the entire process worldwide.

NOTE

1. Adam Smith, *An Inquiry into the Nature and Causes of the Wealth of Nations* (Chicago: University of Chicago Press, 1976), 159.

CHAPTER 2

Customs Expertise

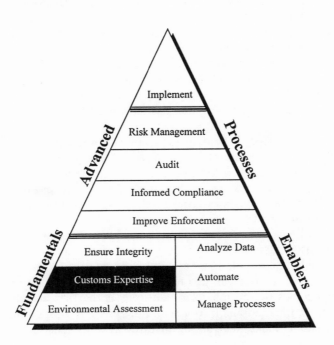

*We make the claim that Japanese companies have been successful be-
cause of their expertise at "organizational knowledge creation." By
organizational knowledge creation we mean the capability of a company as a whole to create new knowledge, disseminate it throughout
the organization and embody it in products, services, and systems.*
—Ikujiro Nonaka and Hirotaka Takeuchi,
The Knowledge-Creating Company[1]

In Chapter 1 we looked at the need for an assessment of the environment and
a self-assessment of customs performance including the level of expertise of
customs personnel. Here we will examine the following dimensions of customs expertise and training: (1) the importance of customs training, (2) the
subject matter of training, (3) sources of training, and (4) the training plan.

IMPORTANCE OF CUSTOMS TRAINING

Training is an investment in the organization and its employees. It is an obligation of the organization and management to provide its employees with the tools
needed to carry out the mission and goals of the agency. Training is one of those
tools. In fact, training is the most important tool and resource an organization
provides to its personnel. In an organization such as customs, with its wide range
of responsibility and complexity, it is imperative that employees are provided
training opportunities that span their entire career, from entry to retirement, and
from the fundamentals of customs to the most advanced aspects of customs technique, practice, procedure, and law. Too frequently, when budgets are tight and
workloads are increasing, training funds are reduced. In fact, in these situations,
training and a professional workforce are vital and failing to provide it can have
long-term detrimental consequences for the organization.

Quality in customs can be defined as accuracy, uniformity, and certainty in
customs actions and decisions. This can only be achieved by a customs organization that has a competency in training and supplements that training with systems
that provide customs officers with timely, accurate, and pertinent information.

The professionalism of customs officers is a reflection on the nation. Customs decisions and actions are not only scrutinized at the port in the country
of importation but also examined in the light of treatment for identical goods
and processes around the world. If customs processing of merchandise (or
conveyances or passengers) is not consistent with world standards for classification, valuation, determination of origin, and procedure, this fact soon becomes known by the international community. Inconsistencies become even
more visible as duty rates fall, just-in-time systems become more prevalent,
and trade becomes more globalized. Customs is the first and most visible
presence for all international travelers and traders. For all these reasons it is
vital that customs make the training investment in the customs officer, the
organization's most valuable asset.

Training begins with recruitment. Unlike professions such as medicine and law, in which new recruits enter the organization after years of specialized university training, newly recruited customs officers ordinarily have no background in customs. Selection of the proper personnel is therefore essential. Testing, background investigation, checking of records and references from previous employment, interviewing, and review of academic achievement are all steps that can ensure applicants make good customs officers. Recruits are the input to the training process. High-quality personnel with a capacity and eagerness for learning combined with an aggressive and professional training program will yield a workforce equal to the demanding requirements of a world-class customs organization. In addition, these officers must be provided with a salary and compensation structure commensurate with a position of honor and trust. It should be a goal of the recruitment process to develop a workforce that will be a source of pride to the nation.

SUBJECT MATTER OF TRAINING

The breadth and scope of customs responsibilities are such that most customs administrations develop specific occupational classifications to perform the variety of customs functions. The customs workforce and organization is typically segmented into classifications that develop specialties and specialized knowledge in classification and value, inspection, audit, enforcement, investigation, entry control, technical areas such as information technology and laboratory sciences, and support functions. Basic training for these categories of employees should be geared to developing an esprit de corps among new employees, a common understanding of the goals of the organization, and how each category or classification contributes to these goals. A common core curriculum for entry-level employees should therefore include segments on the history of customs, the values of the organization, the mission and goals of the agency, and the code of conduct. This training provides an understanding of the importance of customs to the nation and the economy, and the need for customs to support other agency requirements at the border. Basic training should also outline requirements for appearance, and provide guidance on courtesy and dealing with the public. These are fundamentals that every customs officer should know and have in common with all other customs officers nationally and, ultimately, worldwide. The goal is to create a sense of pride, purpose, and unity in an organization devoted to a clear mission, shared vision, and common goals.

The next level of training is in the area of specific occupational training. The purpose of this training is to provide the fundamental skills in a particular customs discipline such as commodity specialist, inspector, investigator, or auditor. Some customs organizations are experimenting with a generalist type position or cross-training of personnel in the various disciplines. The idea of a customs officer who is trained in every discipline and who serves time in every specialty before selecting an area of specialization is a good one. This type of cross-training increases understanding among the various occupations and appreciation of how the various skills must be linked together to achieve organizational goals. In the long term, it also increases cohesiveness and cooperation within the organization. Some customs administrations develop so much pride within a particular discipline that it results in organizational divisiveness, unhealthy competition, and confusion on the part of the public and industry. Good training in the goals of the overall organization and how each segment contributes to these goals helps promote interagency cooperation. Balancing the need for common understanding and cooperation among disciplines is no easy task. Periodic rotation of personnel and cross-training combined with interoffice projects, interdisciplinary teams, and management focus on the overall organizational goals can help provide the necessary balance between the need for specialized in-depth knowledge on the one hand and the need for internal cooperation on the other.

The objective of entry-level training is to start the process of creating experts in every aspect of customs law, value, classification, origin, inspection, procedure, and enforcement. At the successful conclusion of formal entry-level classroom training, which would include a written test of competency, the student will be assigned an entry-level position. In this position the new employee should be assigned a mentor who will be responsible for developing the employee through a series of assignments that will develop all the skills necessary for the junior employee to achieve expert status. This period of on-the-job training should be supplemented by periodic formal training classes to develop specific skills. This combination of formal classroom and on-the-job training through mentors should continue until the employee masters all skills and becomes eligible to mentor others.

Training in customs is a process that never ends. This is because there is not only so much to learn, but also because of the changes continually reshaping customs. By the year 2000, for example, the WCO and WTO will have developed new rules of origin that will eventually need to be mastered and implemented by every customs administration throughout the world. This is an enormous undertaking that will provide rules for determining the origin of everything on the planet. New regional trade agreements likewise require members of these trading blocs to learn the new entitlements made available as a result of the accord. Prudent customs leaders must monitor such activities to update training programs and prepare for implementation.

World and government leaders, importers and exporters, and domestic industry have every right to expect that their customs administrations will obtain and maintain world-class expertise in every aspect of customs law, regulation, and procedure. A first-class formal training program supplemented by on-the-job training is a requirement to meet these expectations. This cycle of formal classroom training, mentorship, and on-the-job training must be repeated throughout the employee's career.

In addition to the traditional customs area of expertise, customs must provide appropriate training in related areas. For example, leadership, management training, automation, data analysis, measurement, statistics, problem solving, and risk management are related disciplines which supplement and complement expert customs knowledge. Over time, employees will take pride in their expertise and learning will be a continuous process. Of particular importance at times of turbulent change is training in leadership and change management. This type of training provides a measure of support and certainty for the organization and its employees in the difficult process of transition and transformation.

SOURCES OF TRAINING

In an ideal world, there would be an International Customs Training Academy, managed by the WCO, at which all customs officers would be trained. Universal centralized training would ensure uniform training in all customs disciplines worldwide by a faculty of internationally recognized experts. While this ideal may never be realized, customs administrations should turn to the WCO for assistance with training. The WCO maintains a cadre of experts on customs training to assist customs organizations determined to increase their professionalism through training. In the absence of the International Customs Training Academy, there are several steps that could be taken by the WCO to upgrade international customs training. These steps would require financial support to the WCO by the advanced economies or by the private sector. These steps would include satellite training on issues ranging from entry level to advanced to specialized training. A series of videotapes could be developed and made available to all customs administrations that would provide the best training in every entry-level area of customs, such as value, classification, and procedures. Computer-based training that would enable every customs officer worldwide to proceed with training at the pace and in the area most needed is now feasible. These suggestions would require substantial financial investment in the WCO for course development and equipment. The outcome, of course, would be increased uniformity, accuracy, and certainty in customs procedures, an action which would, in turn, substantially decrease the cost of international trade transactions. Similar courses could be developed for businesses involved in international trade for their customs managers. These courses could be done in partnership between the WCO and the business community (e.g., the International Chamber of Commerce).

As an alternative to the International Customs Training Academy, the creation of Regional Customs Training Academies under the auspices of the regional WCO bodies and regional trading groups such as NAFTA and ASEAN could be considered. These organizations could be supplemented with support from industry. Joint customs and industry training could also be considered at this level. An innovation that ought to be pursued by governments is having the WCO certify national training to be sure that it is up to international standards.

Until such time as more opportunities for international training materialize, it will be necessary for each customs to develop its own training capabilities. Regardless of future international training facilities and capabilities, it will always be the responsibility of individual customs services to train their own employees. To accomplish this, each customs agency should establish its own customs academy and cadre of experts in customs law, regulation, and procedure. Each customs service must establish its own curriculum and training requirements from entry level to senior level. These formal training requirements should be supplemented by on-the-job training, mentors, training video tapes, and computer-based training. The WCO should be the first stop for training support and guidance. Other customs administrations can frequently be an additional source of training.

A mechanism for coordinating agencywide training requirements of customs is the training committee. The training committee would be established by the top management of customs, and include representation of every major office and function. The training committee would oversee the development and implementation of a training plan.

THE TRAINING PLAN

A well-trained customs workforce is an absolute necessity to carry out the mission of customs. A training plan can provide the framework and road map for achieving the goal of a well-trained workforce expert in every aspect of customs law, regulation, procedure, and process. The training plan would do the following:

- establish priorities for training (i.e., subject areas that are most critical, such as classification and value)
- determine which classes of employee should be trained first, by occupation series as well as basic, mid-level, or advanced
- determine site and type of training (i.e., centralized, on-the-job, formal classroom, videotape, satellite)
- establish a training budget
- monitor progress and results in terms of quantity and quality of training

The training committee should be composed of top managers representing each major office of customs. To address fast-changing conditions, a training plan should be produced annually and derived from organization priorities and needs of the organization. For execution, the training committee should oversee the actions of the training division, often located in the office of human resources, and make use of formal training organizations, foundations, and universities for important specialized training in leadership and change management.

CONCLUSION

A well-trained workforce is absolutely essential in order to achieve the goals of the customs administration. Customs should develop a training plan, establish a training committee, create a training organization, and institute a training academy to accomplish its training goals. In view of the fact that the laws and procedures that customs executes are international in scope, the customs administration should seek guidance and support from the WCO to ensure accurate and uniform execution of international customs conventions. A training budget and top management support for the training function is essential. Over the long term, the possibility of the WCO certifying national customs training should be considered in order to ensure the quality and uniformity of worldwide customs training and to elevate the level of customs expertise on a global basis.

Recommendations from Chapter 2

- Establish a recruitment process that recruits customs officers of highest character and integrity and greatest aptitude and competence to perform at a high level.
- Pay a salary that can attract the highest caliber recruits and reduce any temptation to bribery or corruption.
- Establish a training committee to oversee the training process, determine training needs and priorities, and provide funds for training.
- Conduct a training needs assessment and develop a training plan.
- Ensure that entry-level training provides a strong foundation in the mission, goals, values, priorities, and code of conduct and the need for teamwork among various customs disciplines.
- Develop training plans from entry level to intermediate to senior levels.
- Develop on-the-job training capability to supplement formal classroom training and a mentor program for senior employees to develop junior-level employees.
- Establish a competence in customs training and an academy devoted to customs training.
- Call upon the World Customs Organization for training from inception of the training process.
- Have universities and other learning institutions review training plans, assess their effectiveness, and provide specialized training in leadership and change management.

Actions for Global Customs Managers for Chapter 2

All customs partners in the import and export process should be able to rely upon the competence of customs. Customs knowledge of classification, value, origin, procedure, and related customs and trade matters is the core competence of customs. This core competence and the integrity of the customs institution and its officers are the foundation upon which the national and international trade system are built. In turn, customs has every right to expect that other participants in the trade process are familiar with the general system and expert in their specific areas. Customs should conduct seminars, town meetings, and training for importers, exporters, brokers, carriers, and other government agencies as part of a process to develop competence, trust, and confidence in the system as well as each other. While most customs organizations have a capacity for training, many have their own academy, and all are served by the WCO, industry has no comparable capability to train their customs managers and practitioners. This is a problem or opportunity that could be addressed internationally by the ICC to develop a plan to ensure the competence and expertise of industry in customs matters.

Best practices in international trade are the international standards and conventions agreed upon by the international trade organizations. By definition, these practices should be the same around the world. Customs officials may therefore reasonably expect multinational traders to be competent and expert in the import and export process, or to rely on experts (i.e., brokers, freight forwarders, and consultants) to ensure that their systems and imports are in compliance with all international and national standards. When the competence of customs converges with the competence of its partners in a system based on international standards, the result is world-class customs service.

The private sector has a large stake and big role in the international system of trade. Business can contribute to improving the process in a variety of ways, including the following:

- engaging with customs at all levels in a partnership to improve the process
- attending and participating with customs in international, regional, and national meetings on customs and trade issues
- developing global expertise within the company on customs practice and procedures
- developing expertise in traditional customs practice, such as classification, value, and origin, as well as more recent customs practices, such as audit and risk management
- exploring options for training for customs managers in the business community
- considering the development of an international customs training academy for industry participants in trade matters

These actions hold the promise of significant short- and long-term benefits for industry. In the short term, well-trained industry counterparts to customs will help ensure that duty, customs sanctions, and delays at the border can be minimized. In the long term, the entire international trading system can be streamlined, saving multinational traders time and billions of dollars.

NOTE

1. Ikujiro Nonaka and Hirotaka Takeuchi, *The Knowledge-Creating Company* (New York: Oxford University Press, 1995), viii.

CHAPTER 3

Ensure Integrity

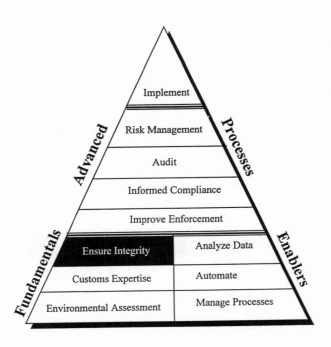

Beyond these economic implications, broader social and political costs derive from the corrupting and intimidating influence of drug trafficking in many areas of the world. Not only does drug traffickers' presence and behavior undermine the authority of government institutions, but in some cases they prevent it from being properly established. The vital process of nations building becomes stalled, if not derailed, in the process.

—Paul B. Stares,
Global Habit: The Drug Problem in a Borderless World[1]

The twin pillars upon which every modern customs administration is built are customs expertise and unquestioned organizational integrity. In Chapter 2 we explored approaches to continuous customs learning. In this chapter we will address the following elements of a comprehensive customs integrity program: (1) importance of integrity, (2) the Peruvian Customs story, (3) the integrity program plan, (4) the integrity checklist, and (5) the relationship between integrity and other aspects of ICMP.

IMPORTANCE OF INTEGRITY

Customs is one of the most rewarding career opportunities to serve one's country. Customs officers protect the health, wealth, safety, and environment of the nations and people they serve. They collect huge sums of revenue, prevent the smuggling of narcotics and other contraband, enforce numerous laws for other government agencies, and help boost economic prosperity by creating the appropriate climate for trade, travel, and tourism at the nation's borders. As transnational crime becomes a larger and larger problem, the importance of customs enforcement and integrity increases and customs vulnerability to breeches of integrity become more frequent and intense.

The important responsibilities of customs create huge demands and introduce temptations and vulnerabilities unmatched in any other occupation. Guns, drugs, money, and contraband in quantities that can only be imagined by the general public are handled by customs officers every day. Unfortunately, and all too often, some customs officers succumb to these temptations. In fact, some customs organizations are so populated with corrupt officers that the entire customs administration is deemed corrupt.

The Fiscal Affairs Department of the International Monetary Fund cites the following as the most important factors that lead to lack of integrity in the administration of duties and taxes:

- complex and restrictive tax and foreign trade systems that lead to rent seeking and corrupt behavior
- high tax and tariff rates

- exemptions
- complex bureaucratic procedures
- weak control systems
- lack of effective disciplinary measures
- lack of professionalism

Appendix D contains the IMF paper, "Practical Measures to Promote Integrity in Customs Administrations."

Transparency International, headquartered in Berlin, Germany, with chapters in over sixty countries, is addressing the general issue of corruption in business and government at national and international levels, going so far as to rate countries by the level of corruption. The United Nations and World Trade Organization are also addressing bribery and corruption in business and government worldwide. The World Customs Organization hosted an extensive dialogue on customs corruption in Tanzania that resulted in the Arusha Declaration (see Appendix E). International organizations, national governments, and customs have now fortunately begun to directly address the corruption problem in government in general and in customs in particular.

Customs corruption is not only a violation of the public trust. It can now result in severe economic damage to the nation. It opens the door to organized crime, drains national revenue in the loss of duty, and results in additional losses of revenues and taxes as businesses avoid a corrupt customs. New technologies in telecommunications, transportation, and manufacturing mean that businesses can operate anywhere and will decide not to operate in countries where the customs system is viewed as corrupt. For all these reasons, and because it is the right thing to do, it is in the best interest of governments and customs administrations to ensure that their customs service and personnel meet the highest standards of honor and integrity. It is also essential that the integrity and honesty of customs and its personnel are maintained and monitored because temptations to bow to corruption are ever-present in the customs arena. While every customs service is always vulnerable to the instances of corruption and most deal with them promptly and severely when they arise, it is essential that customs ensure that there is no systemic corruption in the agency. Without this commitment to triumph over corruption, no system of customs reform and modernization can succeed.

PERUVIAN CUSTOMS STORY

Customs administrations around the world increasingly are combating corruption head-on. For example, as part of its modernization program the government of Peru took aim at corruption. With the support of President Alberto Fujimori, Peruvian customs adopted a program "to professionalize, moralize, and modernize." Seventy percent of the workforce was removed from Peruvian customs as a result of problems with corruption or competence. Peru cited the "political will" to address corruption as a major factor in the success of their modernization program. In addition to removing employees, Peruvian Customs established a code of conduct, simplified procedures for the removal of corrupt employees, developed penalties and sanctions, increased salaries tenfold, raised recruitment standards, required a year of study and training on entrance, and instituted a system of staff rotation.

Peru is an excellent example of the transformation that can be achieved by an administration that demonstrates the political will and long-term commitment to reform. Integrity was only one of the issues addressed by Peruvian Customs, but it is enlightening that the other modernization initiatives would have failed without the commitment to integrity.

New Zealand, ranked number one in the world in integrity by Transparency International, also rates very highly in customer service and enforcement. In Chapter 8, we examine in more detail how New Zealand manages its relationship with the business community and maintains the highest integrity.

THE INTEGRITY PROGRAM PLAN

In view of the vulnerabilities to corruption in customs, it is essential that every customs have a program to ensure the integrity of the organization and its personnel. Integrity assurance programs vary in their structure and content. Some countries have independent integrity oversight and investigation components outside customs, and other countries have the integrity oversight within the customs agency itself. In those instances where customs polices itself, there is need for independent outside review and oversight of the integrity function. Regardless of which approach is taken, a comprehensive integrity program should include the following elements:

- a variety of checks to ensure recruitment of personnel of the highest integrity, including finances, personal references, previous employment, interviews, police and criminal checks, and academic records
- an excellent pay and benefits package consistent with a position of honor and trust
- periodic update on the backgrounds of employees
- pre-employment and periodic random drug testing
- integrity training in all agency training programs
- an investigative arm to review and investigate all allegations of integrity violations and to monitor integrity on a proactive basis
- publishing core values that emphasize integrity and ensure that top management provides the proper example by living these core values
- publishing a code of conduct that outlines expectations of employee behavior (see Appendix F for an example)
- publishing a table of discipline for breaches of integrity, security, or conduct and take swift action to punish any violations

- internal controls in all automated and manual systems to prevent violations and to identify and violations that do occur
- an independent audit review function to monitor internal controls
- creative and innovative methods to detect and prevent integrity violations

Vulnerability of customs to corruption is such that it demands a special element of ICMP to establish, maintain, and monitor integrity. Every customs service in the world must concern itself with this issue now and for all time. The first step in ensuring organizational and institutional integrity is to pay a wage that is consistent with a position of honor and trust. The salary of the customs officer should provide a comfortable income for the customs officer and his or her family. It should then be made clear in word, law, and deed that any violation of the position of honor and trust will result in dismissal and disgrace.

INTEGRITY CHECKLIST

In establishing the customs integrity program the following questions should be asked:

- Is there an integrity or security program in our customs administration?
- Is there an organizational unit and manager responsible and solely dedicated to integrity and security?
- Do employees understand the program, the need for integrity, and the consequences of breaches of integrity?
- Is there an outside unit monitoring the program?
- Have our employees in the integrity oversight group been well trained in detecting and investigating possible integrity violations?
- Is there an active integrity awareness program for employees? Is there a published code of conduct? Has the organization embraced a set of values and communicated them to employees in word and by example? Do those values include integrity?
- Do all systems, automated and manual, have built in security checks and controls?
- Are pre-employment background checks performed on all employees? Are these background checks followed up on a periodic basis?
- Do pre-employment checks include drug testing and financial checks?
- Are employees subject to random drug testing and financial checks?
- Is there a security and integrity manual for employees?
- Are there provisions for discipline and dismissal for integrity violations?
- Are employees encouraged to come forward with information on suspected integrity violations?

These questions should be used in the process of establishing or reviewing the integrity and security function in every customs administration.

There are specific actions that must be taken to maintain integrity as well as built in controls in the elements of ICMP. The following sections summarize areas in which elements of ICMP contribute to an environment that fosters integrity and prevents corruption.

Environmental Assessment

The customs environmental assessment provides an opportunity to examine the world around customs for danger signals of corruption. Questions that should be raised in the environmental assessment include the following:

- Where does our country stand on the Transparency International list of corrupt countries?
- Has the government suffered from corruption scandals in the recent past?
- If so, what actions were taken by customs to address the problem?
- Does the government have laws, regulations, controls, and awareness programs to promote honesty, openness, and integrity in government and business?
- Is there a substantial drug trafficking, drug crime, or drug abuse problem in our country?
- Is the country emerging as a bank haven for proceeds of illegal activities?
- Are there problems in the country related to trafficking in international contraband, firearms, child pornography, intellectual property rights, or stolen goods?

The answers to these questions could provide good information both for the leadership and managers of customs and for the unit charged with maintaining integrity and policing for corruption.

Automation

Automation provides the opportunity to prevent some forms of corruption and requires controls to ensure that new forms of corruption do not emerge. For example, the government of Mexico has mandated direct importer deposits to banks of duties prior to the entry of merchandise. This procedure (though it may cause other problems) ensures that the government receives the duties, fees, and taxes without fear that corrupt personnel will pocket some or all of the revenues. Other customs administrations couple a two-stop entry system with a surety system to ensure collection of revenues and reduce opportunities for theft of cash. On the other hand, computers can be abused by employees in selling sensitive information or unauthorized use or modification to commit or cover up a criminal violation. On the whole, automation can be an important asset to a customs organization in maintaining its integrity provided that appropriate controls and checks are built in and monitored closely.

Analyze Import and Travel Data

The analysis of data in customs computers on travel and trade can be an important asset in maintaining customs integrity. Changes in duty collections at a particular port or fluctuations in payments by a particular importer may signal customs management that a problem exists in personnel integrity. Analysis and monitoring can provide early warning to the management of the security function that there may be a problem.

Informed Compliance and Industry Partnership

Customs interaction with industry must be carefully monitored to prevent bribes and other breaches of integrity. In one role customs is a partner with the industry, in another role industry is a supplier to customs, and in another role industry is a beneficiary of customs services. In all cases customs represents the sovereign state and is the collector of revenue on behalf of that government. Customs must not be seen to be providing special favors for one business or industry over another as a result of bribes or other inducement. Legitimate multinational businesses want fair, equal treatment within the law. If they do not fear coming forward, those businesses can help customs police its own integrity and security.

Improve Quality and Manage Processes

Good business process management, like good automated systems, includes internal and management controls to prevent and deter integrity violations. Care should be taken when developing these systems to build in controls to protect integrity and security.

Audit and Account Management

Audit and account management can provide additional controls to ensure that appropriate revenues are collected, particularly from major revenue sources, and to eliminate some opportunities for bribery and corruption. Audit provides an independent review of importers' records and systems that can be a powerful tool to prevent and detect fraud and corruption. Audit is an important competence to ensure revenue collection and to safeguard integrity.

Measure Compliance and Risk Management

Compliance measurement provides an important tool for monitoring integrity. Severe changes in compliance rates or revenue fluctuations in a particular area may provide indications of fraud or corruption. Comparisons among ports with similar workloads should yield similar results. If results deviate, analysis should be performed as to causes.

CONCLUSION

There is no more important function of customs leadership than establishing an environment that promotes the honesty and integrity of customs and its personnel and one that prevents and punishes breaches of integrity and security. Four important steps on the part of management must be taken to fulfill this obligation:

1. Take ownership of the issue
2. Implement ICMP with its integrity checks in each element
3. Institute a strong security and integrity program and unit along the lines described
4. Establish a code of conduct and institutional values that include integrity and ensure that top management leads by example

Some customs administrations around the world are considering the interface of their automated systems. In the long term, the exchange of import and export data between customs organizations would not only streamline the customs process but also act to prevent fraud by importers and eliminate opportunities for bribery and corruption within customs. Such data exchanges should be encouraged to facilitate trade, improve enforcement, and guard against breaches of integrity.

Recommendations from Chapter 3

- Review the integrity rating assigned to your country by Transparency International and consider the implications for your customs administration.
- Review the Arusha Declaration of the WCO and consider the integrity implications for your customs organization.
- Review the organizational structure to ensure accountability for the integrity and security function and modify the organizational structure as appropriate.
- Establish a system of compensation commensurate with a position of honor and trust and sufficient to avoid temptation and vulnerability to corruption.
- Ensure that the recruitment system does adequate background checks to weed out all but the most desirable candidates.
- Include integrity, values, a code of conduct, and a table of discipline in all training at all levels.
- Publish core values that include the highest level of integrity and ensure that all employees starting with top management live by those values.
- Build in internal controls in all manual and automated systems and establish a system of checks and audits to detect possible violations.

Actions for Global Customs Managers for Chapter 3

The international trade community has every right to expect and demand a trade system and environment that is free from corruption. They also have a responsibility to contribute toward building an environment characterized by integrity and ensuring that their own organization is free from the taint of corruption. Surprisingly, few countries prohibit their companies from bribing foreign officials for such things as bids for overseas contracts. Shockingly, some nations allow their companies tax deductions for foreign bribes. Regardless of the current legal status, bribery is morally and ethically wrong and leads to or promotes the continuation of endemic corruption. Cooperation of the entire international community is required to remove corruption and bribery as a factor in the trading system.

Nations must develop the political will to eradicate corruption. A free press and a strong judicial system are necessary first steps. Business should be encouraged to step forward to expose corrupt practices. International organizations which have taken stands against corruption, such as Transparency International, the WCO, the WTO, and the IMF, should be supported by the private sector. Individual companies can greatly influence the climate of integrity by several means:

- supporting the efforts of national officials to establish and maintain integrity in those countries exhibiting the political will to do so
- avoiding altogether or minimizing trade and investment in those countries which have not taken measures to reform
- establishing values and codes of conduct that make it clear that bribery and corruption will not be tolerated
- developing systems and internal controls to identify problems with bribery and corruption
- removing employees who violate the policies on honesty and integrity
- cooperating with law enforcement entities by providing information on suspicious behavior
- cooperating with law enforcement authorities on corruption investigations

Creating a climate of honesty and integrity requires the cooperation of government and business. It requires political will and commitment from the top in government organizations as well as business. It is a long-term, never-ending process. Those countries determined to combat and conquer corruption will find willing partners in international organizations, and must be supplemented by the support of business.

NOTE

1. Paul B. Stares, *Global Habit: The Drug Problem in a Borderless World* (Washington, D.C.: The Brookings Institution, 1996), 97.

PART II

THE ENABLERS

CHAPTER 4

Manage Processes

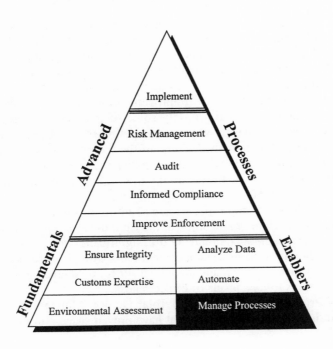

But what about the success stories of the new management? Certainly there have been some, but they have happened because managers have used their ingenuity to adopt to new ideas, such as TQM, to the particular contexts of their companies. When tailored to fit specific situations, and often changed beyond recognition, these ideas proved invaluable. This is pragmatic management at its best.

—Nitin Nohria and James D. Berkely,
"What Ever Happened to the Take-Charge Manager?"[1]

Business Process Management and Total Quality Management are important management tools that, along with automation and data analysis, provide the foundation for new levels of effectiveness, efficiency, and achievement for customs organizations employing them. The three elements of ICMP described in this section, process management, automation, and data analysis, are so important that we refer to them as enablers since they enable, or make possible, approaches to increasing customs effectiveness that were never before possible. In this chapter the concept of process management in general is introduced, customs processes are addressed more specifically, and the relationship between process management and other aspects of ICMP are discussed.

THE CONCEPT OF PROCESS MANAGEMENT

The past ten years have witnessed a greater introduction of new management tools and techniques than any other time in history. Managers have been overwhelmed by a tidal wave of books, seminars, and magazines describing the new management. Reengineering, best practices, benchmarking, empowerment, one-minute management, learning organization, knowledge creation, process mapping, business process improvement, work-out, bottom-up, top-down, vertical, and horizontal are only some of the terms and buzzwords touted by their promoters as providing a competitive edge. A new industry of management gurus has flourished. Some of the theories and strategies have proven weak or even foolish. Some of the "experts" seem in retrospect not so wise. A new profession has grown around the ridicule of management fads and "flavors of the month."

On the other hand, if the proper management innovation is introduced in the right way in the right organization at the right time, taking into consideration the context and organizational culture, significant improvements can be realized. Combining these new management tools with advances in information technology and statistical and analytical skills could leverage some customs organizations to new levels of effectiveness.

Business Process Management and Total Quality Management are two management improvement processes that have proven successful in increasing organizational effectiveness. To organizations committed to change and modernization, BPM and TQM provide vehicles for introducing and managing change over the long term. BPM and TQM are not short-term fixes. In fact, one of the reasons for including BPM and TQM in ICMP is that they provide the necessary commitment for a long-term process of change and improvement. Businesses and government agencies have begun identifying their "processes" and developing systematic approaches to improving these processes.

A *process* is defined as a "systematic series of actions directed to some end" or a "collection of activities that takes one or more inputs and adds value to that input for a customer." In the case of customs, the "customer" may be the general public, a carrier, a broker, an importer, or a tourist, among others. Process management differs from traditional approaches to organizing work in several ways. For example, whereas most organizations have tended to organize and manage by occupational series or functional specialty, process management requires that our perspective of work be broadened to visualize a stream of work, or process, that flows from inputs (merchandise, consignees, or passengers) to finished products (cleared goods and passengers in compliance with customs and other agency laws) in a timely fashion at minimal cost to government and industry. With process management, organizations view their work flow horizontally across organizational lines and view those processes from end to end as a whole. Processes are continually reviewed and improved. Old methods and procedures are systematically challenged to ensure that they are still relevant. Unnecessary work is pruned. Process management thus results in a simplified, streamlined work flow.

CUSTOMS PROCESSES

Customs administrations have typically organized and operated along functional lines and on a vertical basis in what management experts and consultants call "silos" or "smoke stacks." In this scenario, each organizational component in customs is responsible for a particular area of customs processing. No organizational unit or manager is responsible for the entire operation except the commissioner or director general. With this approach it is possible and likely that one or more customs functions could achieve their individual organizational goals without the overall goals of customs compliance being met. "Hand-offs" between functions—for example, between an inspector or commodity specialist—can result in delays and missed opportunities. No one sees the "big picture" or views the process as a whole except the very top management. In process management, this vertical way of looking at our work is replaced by a horizontal viewpoint.

With process management the core processes are viewed from an integrated perspective from end to end (see Figure 4.1). All the skills, resources, and expertise of the entire organization are brought to bear on the process in an integrated fashion. Under process management a process owner is named

Figure 4.1
Process Management

who is responsible for the entire process and ensuring that the overall agency goals are met. Crossfunctional interdisciplinary teams are created to solve problems and manage the processes. For example, customs receives inputs in the form of cargo or entry documents from suppliers, brokers, or importers and processes them to ensure they are in compliance with customs laws resulting in an output of cleared cargo in compliance for a customer (i.e., the importer and the public). The functional office and occupational skills are still employed, but in a disciplined manner, in crossfunctional teams, and with the overall compliance goal of the organization in mind.

Overseeing this entire process is a process owner who takes the leadership for every aspect of the process from end to end. Under process management, functional managers clearly see their role in the process in helping the organization to achieve its overall goal, rather than the limited goals of their individual functional area. Everyone in the organization is now focused on the overall goal, in this case delivery of cargo in compliance with customs laws on a timely basis. The measures are clear: cost, quality, and speed where quality is defined as cargo that is accurately and uniformly classified, valued, and in compliance with all customs requirements. When combined with TQM and best practices or benchmarking, customs organizations can move systematically to consistently higher levels of compliance with greater facilitation of cargo and passengers at lower costs.

Business Process Management begins with the identification of customs processes. While BPM may be new to customs as a formal discipline, customs has always had processes or a series of procedures. Over time, processes have developed for handling cargo and passengers, for the classification and appraisal of goods, and for the collection of revenue. As problems and opportunities arise, customs has created new processes and developed organizations around these processes. The problem arises in that these processes become fragmented and disconnected. Customs officers fail to see the import or passenger process as a whole. This fragmentation and disconnection results in time delays, poor communication, and the failure to see the objective of the organization as a whole. They see their role as accomplishing a series of procedures or steps in a predetermined order, not as an integrated process for achieving an important organizational goal. Viewed from the outside, importers and carriers and other users of customs services see an organization that is fragmented and compartmentalized, and one that is characterized by

Figure 4.2
Overall Process Structure

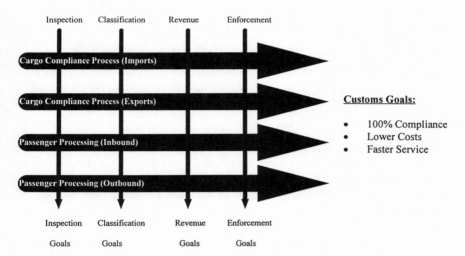

poor internal communication. Importers frequently feel they are "getting the run around" and that "the organization does not speak with one voice." Process management can remedy these complaints.

Customs' processes typically include a cargo process and a passenger process. Some customs services also have processes for export and processes for passengers exiting the country. Under this scenario the overall process structure would look as illustrated in Figure 4.2.

In each process a process owner would be named and process improvement teams would be formed. A goal is established to achieve 100-percent compliance with reduced costs and improved processing times. Measurement and control systems are built into the process. The processes would each be "mapped" or flow diagrammed to determine areas where processes could be improved by introducing controls or eliminating redundant steps.

It is recommended that one process be selected for pilot test of the process management technique. Alternatively, a program could be initiated to convert to process management for all operational or support processes. If all processes are defined and implemented simultaneously, it is recommended that one receive priority attention in terms of budget and management oversight.

PROCESS MANAGEMENT AND ICMP

Converting to process management impacts every aspect of the organization. The following sections describe the interaction between process management and other elements of ICMP.

Automation

Automation is essential to attaining the full benefits of ICMP. Each process should be automated and each process owner should be linked with a project manager responsible for automation of the process. The process owner and project manager will work as a team to improve and streamline the process. This link between process management and automation is one of the keys to leveraging the organization to new heights of effectiveness and efficiency.

Analyze Import and Trade Data

Each process owner and member of the process team will use analysis of the data in the automated system to improve compliance and streamline the processes. The data in customs automated systems on international trade are a national treasure. The ability to manipulate these data is the key to leveraging performance of customs to higher levels of compliance.

Audit and Account Management

Audit and account management will, over time, lead to an interface of processes between customs and industry as well as other government agencies and other customs services. Ultimately, customs will (1) receive export data from carriers, exporters, and other customs services, (2) process these data through its automated systems to achieve compliance, and (3) deliver the data and cleared cargo to the automated systems of importers and importing carriers. This same process will be repeated on the export side and developed for inbound and outbound passengers as well. This will be the seamless international system, the international trade and travel superhighway of the future. It will represent the interface and automation of all customs, carriers, importers, exporters, and support players.

Informed Compliance and Industry Partnerships

Process owners inform industry of the processes, publish the process map, and include industry in the development and design of the processes in order to enable industry to comply. The linkage and alignment of customs processes with industry processes and systems is a key to the seamless flow of goods across international borders.

Improve Enforcement

BPM and TQM enhance customs enforcement in several ways:

- automation and process improvement save resources that can be reinvested in compliance and enforcement

- process improvement requires internal controls and checks that improve security and enhance integrity of processes
- process improvement teams include enforcement personnel, which increases understanding of processes and boosts security safeguards

By establishing processes to handle all of the legitimate commercial business of customs, the organization is able to focus its attention and resources on criminals, violations, and deliberate noncompliance, thus increasing compliance and enforcement effectiveness.

Maintain Integrity

Integrity of the organization is enhanced through BPM and TQM because internal controls and security safeguards are built into all automated and manual processes and audits are periodically conducted to ensure the integrity of the system.

Measure Compliance and Manage Risk

BPM and TQM establishment a framework for measurement of customs effectiveness never before possible. For the first time, customs and its employees can measure progress in meeting customs compliance and facilitation goals. This ability to achieve measurable progress toward important goals is a motivating force for the organization and its employees. Variations in compliance over time and among ports may signal the need for corrective action or a potential integrity or security problem.

SUMMARY

BPM and TQM are successful business techniques that have application for strengthening and modernizing customs. Every element of ICMP is enhanced by the discipline introduced by BPM and TQM. The discipline of Business Process Management and improvement ensures that all the improvements achieved by ICMP are maintained and built upon over the years. Business Process Management and improvement represents the approach that multinational businesses are using to link and integrate their global processes. In the long term, customs organizations will link and integrate the customs process nationally at all ports of entry, internationally with other customs services, and with the international private sector through global customs management. This will be the seamless international trade superhighway, resulting in high compliance, uniform worldwide customs processes, systems, and service, lower cost for compliance to customs and industry, and faster clearance for legitimate shipments. Finally, BPM and TQM represent the long-term commitment that organizations must make to continuous improvement.

Recommendations from Chapter 4

- Investigate the possibility of introducing BPM and TQM to the customs environment. Of course, BPM and TQM are not a quick fix. They represent a long-term commitment and should not be initiated if the organization is not committed from the very top. It is highly recommended that a consultant with a proven track record of achievement and expertise be utilized to support the organization in introducing BPM and TQM.

- Use an Executive Improvement Team (EIT) to provide oversight, guidance, and support to the entire process.

- Train personnel at all levels and include other government agencies in the training program. Involve suppliers and industry in the process.

- Identify core business processes and major support processes that represent the work of the organization.

- Decide on a first process as a pilot project and make a commitment to process improvement.

- Appoint a process owner to lead the process from end to end, including process flow charting, process redesign, automation, and measurement.

- Ensure that customs processes are developed with the goal of alignment of those processes with the processes of other government agencies, international business, and other customs administrations.

Actions for Global Customs Managers for Chapter 4

The original concept of TQM was to improve internal processes. Over a period of time, with the introduction of sophisticated logistics management systems and just-in-time delivery systems, the objective became to link and synchronize the processes of suppliers, manufacturers, transportation providers, and customs to achieve greater efficiencies and savings. With global trade in merchandise exceeding the $5 trillion mark, more and more companies are going international, underscoring the need to integrate customs and other government agency systems in their logistics planning. Even intrafirm trade that is international, which now accounts for over 30 percent of world trade in goods, must factor customs requirements into their system to achieve seamless processing. The express courier industry was a pioneer in recognizing the necessity of working with customs to streamline processes worldwide.

If you were asked to draw a chart of your organization and its relationships, chances are you would find that you placed your organization at the center of the chart. Most organizations place themselves at the middle of the universe and are startled to find themselves at the periphery of everyone else's chart. Between customs and industry, the WCO has provided a useful array of tools to make the interface of government and business systems as fast, predictable, uniform, and mutually beneficial as possible. These include systems for the uniform treatment in classification, value, procedures, and, soon, origin, as well as recommendations for automation and common computer and communications, protocols, and syntax. It is tempting, however, for business and government alike to favor in-house proprietary systems, processes, and protocols in which there is a large investment and which are more efficient and cost effective in the short term. For the long term, converting to worldwide standards such as UNEDIFACT and linking government and industry processes together is the key to the worldwide seamless system that can unlock tens of billions of dollars in savings each year. As a start in the direction of realizing these savings, customs partners can follow the lead of the pioneers in the field by doing the following:

- work cooperatively with all parties, including customs, to design processes to link government and industry systems into a worldwide integrated system
- support the concept of making customs the focal point for coordinating all government border systems, processes, and requirements
- resist the temptation to optimize all processes at the national and local levels at the expense of the international
- adopt all international standards and protocols for computers and communications (e.g., UNEDIFACT)
- work cooperatively with customs to support their missions of raising compliance levels and improving enforcement for all government requirements at international borders
- recognize that export and import are related processes that provide the foundation for an integrated worldwide trading system

As confidence and trust are established between customs and industry based on an understanding of their respective and legitimate needs, and as respect is developed based on mutual recognition of competence and integrity, customs and industry can move to build integrated systems and processes to the benefit of both.

NOTE

1. Nitin Nohria and James D. Berkely, "What Ever Happened to the Take-Charge Manager?" *Harvard Business Review*, January–February 1994, 131.

CHAPTER 5

Automate

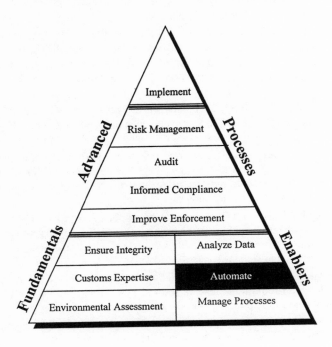

Automation is an enabling technology for customs administra-
tions committed to modernizing and improving their efficiency and
effectiveness. Top management oversight of the automation initia-
tive is essential to ensure that the full potential of information
technology is realized. Without a commitment from the top auto-
mation can prove to be a costly disaster. With top management
commitment, support, and direction information technology can
propel customs to new levels of effectiveness.

—James W. Shaver, Secretary General,
World Customs Organization[1]

For many years the promise of automation had exceeded its performance. Many automation initiatives in government and industry proved to be costly failures. After decades of investment, experimentation, and frustration, automation and information technology is now providing many of the benefits envisioned by pioneers in the field. The future of customs administrations lies in automation and information technology. Automation is the key to dealing with exponential increases in trade, travel, and tourism. Information technology is also the key to increasing the effectiveness of customs and promoting worldwide uniformity and cooperation among customs administrations.

The power of computers is increasing; their cost is steadily decreasing. Advances in communications technology and the Internet provide new ideas and new opportunities for trade and business on a daily basis. The pace of this change seems to be ever increasing. Even with all these advantages and new breakthroughs in technology, many automation initiatives still fail or provide fewer benefits than originally envisioned. With this in mind, here are some cautionary notes for initiating or expanding an automation project:

- Even though costs of technology are decreasing, the costs for systems development, personnel, and contractors can be deceptively and extremely high. The effort should be planned in such a way that these costs are identified and budgeted.

- Organizations frequently automate existing practices and thus do not capitalize on the full capabilities of the new technology. The automation project should include a complete review of processes and procedures and a redesign of those processes to capture the full benefits of the technology.

- Organizations should adhere to international standards and practices. Customs is an international organization, and so too are its counterparts in industry and other customs organizations. To make the worldwide system of international trade work, worldwide systems and standards must be adopted.

- Automation must include all stakeholders. Importers, exporters, carriers, and employees all have an important stake in the old system and the new system, and should be included in the process from the beginning.

- Automation should include the requirements of other agencies with responsibility for imports, such as agriculture, food, safety, and environment.

Every one of these possible pitfalls can and has been overcome. Automation and the application of information technology has been spectacularly effective for many customs administrations. There is no reason to fail when the factors outlined are taken into consideration and a good plan is developed and implemented. In this chapter, we discuss (1) planning for automation and information technology, (2) designing and developing the system, and (3) implementing and managing the system.

PLANNING AND INFORMATION TECHNOLOGY

Automation impacts every aspect of customs. Consequently, most customs organizations employ some form of automated system. These systems range from the fundamental to the very sophisticated. Because of the rapid pace of change in technology and the rapid rate of growth of international trade, it is necessary for all customs services to periodically review their automation requirements. Because of the vital importance of automation to customs, this review of automation and information technology needs should be conducted at a very high level. To begin the automation planning process, the Director General or Commissioner of customs should appoint a senior customs official to conduct a study of the customs information requirements. Since automation impacts every aspect of customs, every functional area of customs should be represented on this committee. The information requirements committee should be given a charter to do the following:

- complete the study in a specified time period (e.g., six months)
- provide a comprehensive report on all current and future (up to five years) information needs
- obtain the advice and input of information technology experts
- include industry and other government agency requirements in the planning process
- become familiar with computer and communications technology capabilities and potential
- review the customs strategic plan, environmental assessment, and data analysis needs
- consider the advantages and disadvantages of in-house development, contractor development, and turnkey systems development
- ensure that all proposed systems and subsystems are in conformance with international standards
- be alert to new opportunities and capabilities provided by technology and avoid automating existing procedures when advanced processes are made possible

An effective automation and information technology planning process not only looks at customs in terms of what it is now, but also, and more important, it looks at customs as it might and can be. In that regard the process must work hand in hand with the Business Process Management and Total Quality Management approaches described in Chapter 4. BPM and TQM require a rigorous flow diagram of current processes and a consideration of new processes from incremental improvement to total reengineering. As such, BPM and TQM are the sources of innovation and redesign of work that will be the foundations for new automated systems and new information requirements. It is this marriage of BPM and TQM with information technology that provides many of the benefits of computer and communications technology. Most important, customs systems development efforts should all culminate in the design of a database and data analysis system that will be the foundation for targeting, selectivity, audit, risk management, and increasing customs compliance.

The review team should also examine the United Nations' ASYCUDA++ system, an automated customs system provided by the United Nations Conference on Trade and Development. While the ASYCUDA++ software is provided free, there are significant costs associated with implementation. ASYCUDA++ is a good system. It is recommended for administrations embarking on automation with limited budgets. It can also provide experience and a transition to more sophisticated systems. The review team should analyze the advantages and disadvantages of the ASYCUDA++ system, including costs versus the development and implementation of a system tailored to the unique requirements of the customs administration.

The product of the review team should be a plan for going forward to meet the customs administration's information-processing needs. This plan should result in the development of a contract proposal to procure hardware and software (a turnkey system), to develop the software in-house on existing hardware or procure new hardware, or to turn to the United Nations for support in implementing ASYCUDA++. Regardless of which approach is taken, the process is not over. It has just begun.

DESIGNING AND DEVELOPING THE SYSTEM

Today's modern automated customs information systems are fast, user-friendly, and powerful. They place tremendous power in the hands of customs and the customs officer. However, there is a cost—in dollars, but also in time, rigor, and hard work—associated with successful design and development. No matter what path is chosen, ASYCUDA++, in-house development, or contract system, functional experts and managers at all levels must devote months and years of effort to ensure that the system envisioned is the system delivered. Turning the project and specifications over to the technical people in the expectation that several months or even years later the specified system will be delivered is a formula for disaster. Expecting integration of complex hardware and software systems nationwide with the flip of a switch is a fantasy. The delivery of hardware and connection of telecommunications facilities is an arduous process. It is not self-implementing, and cannot be left entirely to technical personnel. It is an agency-wide undertaking that requires a team effort with support from the top.

In many organizations, the design and development effort is coordinated through an Information Technology Steering Committee (ITSC). This committee is typically chaired by a senior executive and includes representatives of each functional office. In view of the importance of automation and information technology to every aspect of customs operation, it is recommended that an ITSC be established to provide direction and support to this vital asset. During the design and development phase, the purpose of the ITSC would be to provide overall guidance and direction to the technical staff responsible for systems design and development, establish priorities for implementation derived from the overall organization priorities, and monitor progress and maintain accountability.

The ITSC must provide leadership and support to the initiative because installing and implementing an effective automated customs system represents a major change in the way customs does business. Automation requires a change in the customs culture from the traditional manual processing, transaction-by-transaction approach to one that enables the organization to look at companies, industries, and even countries as a whole. If the transition to the automated processing is not given high-level attention and accompanied by an extensive training program for all employees, the system is destined to fail or produce very limited benefits. In the installation of any new automated system, it is also necessary to look at every aspect of every employee's work to determine how it is impacted by automation and how that job should be changed as the result of automation. At the same time, management should be examining new opportunities as a result of the new automation tool. Examples of questions that should be posed when automation is introduced include the following:

- Are there new positions that should be created to take advantage of the new capabilities (e.g., personnel skilled in data analysis)?
- How should we redesign our work processes to take advantage of automation?
- What functions previously performed manually can now be better performed by the automated system?
- How are the work processes of existing jobs and employees enhanced by the automation?
- What new safeguards can be put in place to protect security, integrity, and revenue?
- What training is needed to ensure the best utilization of new capabilities?
- What linkage must be established with the BPM and TQM initiatives to ensure the greatest benefits of the automation effort?

If these and other questions are not considered in depth, there is a danger that full benefits of automation will not be received or that redundant and parallel work systems will be installed. However, when these issues are given full consideration and there is a thoughtful implementation plan that deals with the fears and concerns of employees and puts automation in the context of the goals of the entire organization, automation will provide the springboard to new levels of effectiveness. At the same time, employee morale and job satisfaction can actually increase as employees can utilize the new tools in making measurable progress toward important goals.

IMPLEMENTING AND MANAGING THE SYSTEM

The costs of automation and the application of information technology are high. The time frame for implementation of the full benefits can be long. However, if the organization perseveres, the benefits will be great. In the long term, the data in the automated system become an important resource for customs. Properly applied, these data become invaluable for customs and business. Properly implemented, the customs automated import system becomes the equivalent of a national utility for importers and exporters. In fact, in the long term, the interface of customs systems around the world becomes the international information superhighway for the movement of goods and trade-related data worldwide. As multinational companies integrate their systems and create seamless systems within the corporation and with their suppliers worldwide, so too must customs organizations link up internationally through telecommunications. The ultimate linkup of integrated automated commercial systems with an international network of interfaced customs systems will achieve the vision of the seamless worldwide system. With automation, customs administration and their counterparts in industry can look at import and export as part of a single process rather than two discrete and unrelated processes. Customs administrations which are not automated or do not incorporate international standards such as UNEDIFACT will be left behind. The availability of modern state-of-the-art customs systems will be taken into consideration as companies make decisions on trade and investment. Future growth and economic prosperity are the issues at stake for customs administrations moving to automation or upgrading their systems to the next generation of technology. As the focal point for the automation of international trade data, customs must now view itself as a supplier of information and services to the trade community and other agencies.

The ITSC role in supporting automation in customs does not end with the design and development phase. In fact, the role of the ITSC increases during and after implementation. During the implementation phase, the ITSC provides support to the technical implementation team in several ways:

- providing visibility to the project throughout the organization
- coordinating with the operational and support offices to ensure they carry out their vital roles in utilizing the new systems
- providing encouragement and leadership as problems arise in implementation and early operation of the system (and there will be problems in implementation)

After the system is implemented, customs leadership (typically through a mechanism such as the ITSC) must continue to provide oversight and support to automation and technology as a new way of doing business. Managing the technology includes the following functions:

- monitoring new developments in technology that can be applied to customs to increase efficiency and effectiveness
- identifying and prioritizing new applications as candidates for customs automation
- reviewing operational procedures to ensure that they have changed and adapted to take advantage of the automation investment
- considering the establishment of new types of positions to take advantage of the new capabilities
- resolving disputes between operational and technical offices on the use of the technology
- identifying new uses for the system as experience is gained in operation
- protecting the privacy, security, and integrity of the system and the organization

The successful automation of customs processes and introduction of information technology will be characterized by continued top-management commitment, which can be provided by the ITSC.

Finally, the leadership of the organization must address the human aspects of automation. Many employees and managers will fear or resist automation. They may see it as a threat to their job security. They may want to continue old practices and procedures that do not take full advantage of the opportunities provided by the automated systems. Management must address these issues by training, retraining, and explaining the purpose and rationale for automation and the opportunities it provides for job enrichment, job satisfaction, and higher organizational performance. Of course, these cannot be hollow promises. They must be kept. With persistence and diligence, employees and managers can make this difficult transition from the manual to the automated environment with major benefits to the employee as well as the organization and the community it serves.

CONCLUSION

Automation is not an end in itself. The goal of automation is to move the organization toward the goal of 100-percent compliance with customs laws, while reducing the costs of compliance and reducing processing or cycle time. Investment in automation and information technology is fundamental to all elements of ICMP. The approach described in this chapter is change on a grand scale, change that can transform an organization to achieve new levels of effectiveness. In future chapters, we will return to the subject of information technology, particularly as it pertains to process improvement and more effective customs enforcement and compliance. By automating customs processes, the organization develops a reservoir of information on international trade that is of great value to the nation and to customs. Analysis of these data enables the organization to look at entire companies, industries, and countries. Developing the expertise to analyze these data is the subject of Chapter 6.

Recommendations from Chapter 5

- Make an organizational commitment to modernization of customs based substantially on automation and information technology.
- Link the organization's information technology plan to the process-improvement plans to achieve the greatest impact and benefits.
- Consult outside experts as appropriate in developing the information technology plan. This is essential; current computer and communications technology is too complex and fast changing to go it alone without expert outside assistance.
- Derive the information technology plan from the long-range and strategic plans of the organization and a study of the organization's information needs.
- Consider the installation of ASYCUDA++ as one of the options for the basic customs processing system.
- Establish an Information Technology Steering Committee at a very high level, and use it to guide the development and management of the information technology and automation effort.
- Involve other agencies, employees, and industry in the process from the beginning and ensure that their needs are incorporated in the system.
- Build in security, privacy, and integrity controls to protect the interests of government and industry.
- Consider the benefits of integrating the export and import processes and the long-term potential for interfacing with other customs administrations.
- Ensure that all systems developed are undertaken with an eye toward international integration and interface and use UNEDIFACT standards.

Actions for Global Customs Managers for Chapter 5

Customs administrations around the world are turning to automation and information technology to achieve their mission and goals and to cope with increasing workloads, demands for better service, and pressure for increased enforcement. Developing the automated customs system linking all border locations, meeting the demands of other government agencies, and providing an electronic interface to all members of the trade community is a tall order. While developing the national customs system is a complex undertaking, consider the problems of the multinational company—importer, exporter, or carrier, for example—who must interface with dozens of customs around the world. Some of these customs may be automated, some manual, some sophisticated, some primitive. Some may follow international standards, others may have home-grown proprietary systems. The problem is that each is unique, requiring the truly multinational trader to develop dozens of different, localized systems to meet customs requirements in each country. These unique, proprietary systems contribute to the tens of billions of dollars in unnecessary annual costs and inefficiencies in the multinational trading system.

In theory, automation and international standards for communications interfaces provide the solution. Someday a multinational company headquartered in Jakarta could be preparing entries for all countries out of its central logistics system, or a freight forwarder in Rio de Janeiro could be handling the export requirements of many companies to multiple countries out of one integrated system. In the real world, each country wants to build the world's best customs system. National managers for multinational companies are enticed by the prospect of making their national operation the best in the world. The result is a hodgepodge of systems, all vying for world-class status. In reality, the best system is the system that meets international standards and practices, just as the best procedure is that which is consistent with Kyoto, the best value system is the GATT Value Code, and the best classification system is the Harmonized Tariff System. Ultimately, a global customs system tying together all customs and their trading partners using international standards and exchanging import and export data is the ideal. The following actions are recommended to achieve the potential of automation for facilitating the free flow of merchandise and reducing the costs, barriers, and inefficiencies of international trading systems:

- Engage with customs at the international, regional, and national levels in building customs systems using international standards such a UNEDIFACT.
- Insist that automated customs systems include the border-crossing requirements of all other government agencies.
- Provide customs with advance information and access to business automated systems pertaining to imports and exports.
- Support experiments and prototypes in advanced automation techniques such as the North American Trade Automation Prototype, and the interfaces between New Zealand and Australia and the United States and England.
- Consider the example of the express courier industry, which has provided leadership and tangible support to customs as a path to a standardized worldwide system.

The goal of a worldwide integrated and standardized customs system is attainable. The reward is billions upon billions in annual savings and increased effectiveness for government and industry. Business engagement with customs is the key.

NOTE

1. James W. Shaver, Personal Communication, Brussels, World Customs Organization, 1997.

CHAPTER 6

Analyze Data

*The emerging strategies demand that the skills of analysis should
be given a higher profile, more akin to the recognition afforded
analysis as a basis for professional judgment in the fields of medicine, defense, and intelligence.*
                                   —Malcolm K. Sparrow, *Imposing Duties:
                                   Government's Changing Approach to Compliance*[1]

In Chapters 4 and 5, we reviewed customs processes and customs automation, which set the stage for true customs modernization by enabling customs
to manipulate data in automated systems in ways never before possible. In
this chapter we examine more closely the data that are in the customs domain
and how those data can be leveraged to increase the efficiency and effectiveness of customs operations. The worldwide increase in travel, trade, and tourism is examined in light of the challenges it poses for customs and a new
framework for viewing the customs workload is revealed. Finally, examples
are given of how customs can meet its challenges in revenue collection and
enforcement by sophisticated analysis of information in customs databases.

THE CUSTOMS WORLD AND THE
CUSTOMS CHALLENGE

All goods and people entering—and, in some countries, all goods and people
exiting—must pass through customs and must comply with all customs requirements. Even in the smallest countries, this means that millions of people
and billions of dollars of goods pass through customs, pay duties and taxes,
and meet requirements of other government agencies. Goods and people arrive by air, land, and sea, and customs is responsible for the control and inspection of conveyances as well. In this process, customs works with multiple
players: importers, exporters, brokers, international carriers, domestic carriers, sureties, warehouses, trade zones, and numerous government agencies,
among others.

The customs challenge is to ensure that all goods and travelers enter and
exit in compliance with all customs and government requirements, and that
they do so in an expeditious manner. In many countries trade and travel is
increasing exponentially as governments look upon trade and tourism as en-
gines of economic growth and prosperity. Many customs administrations are
finding that staffing, budget, and resources are not keeping pace with growth
in international travel and trade. There may be a feeling among some customs
administrations and employees that either enforcement and compliance with
customs laws or facilitation and timely processing of goods and passengers
must be sacrificed in order to cope with the tremendous increases in international travel and trade. Complicating this picture even more may be new requirements and demands placed upon customs by new trade agreements,

quotas, or enforcement responsibilities in the areas of narcotics, money laundering, intellectual property rights, the environment, health, or safety.

If this apparent conflict between the demands being placed on customs and the resources available to customs is not resolved, it can have a devastating effect on the morale and performance of customs. Resolving these apparent conflicts between resources and workload and enforcement (compliance) and facilitation is now within reach of every customs organization. However, it requires that customs administrations look at the work of customs from a new perspective and adopt new approaches to addressing the work.

Figure 6.1 illustrates the problem for many customs administrations in dealing with the worldwide growth in travel, trade, and tourism. International transactions are typically doubling every decade, while customs resources remain steady, increase slightly, or even decline. The perceived gap between resources and workload can be 100 percent or more in many countries over the time span of a decade. Closing this gap is a challenge that can be met by innovation, automation, and technology. Data analysis is one of the innovations that can help close the gap.

THE WORK OF CUSTOMS

For decades, indeed for centuries, the work of customs and customs view of its work did not change substantially. Customs work was traditionally reactive. People and goods would present themselves at the border and customs would essentially look upon each passenger and shipment as an entity unto itself. This was particularly true at land borders, where the act of import and export are almost simultaneous and advance information is almost never provided. Goods and people were treated as transactions, and processing was done transaction by transaction supported only by manual files and the memory of customs officers. When trade or travel increased, customs would present data on the additional numbers of passengers and cargo declarations to the

Figure 6.1
The Customs Gap

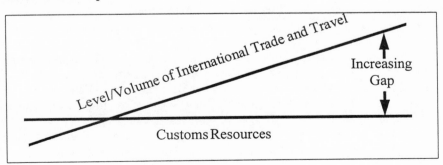

appropriate authorities as proof of the increase in customs workload and request additional resources. This request for funding and personnel would typically be accompanied by data on additional revenues that would be collected, contraband that would be seized, or delays and congestion that would be avoided if the funds were appropriated and the additional employees were brought on board.

In many ways customs viewed its workload as those transactions and its work as the processing of these transactions. In return for doing a reasonable job in processing these transactions and collecting appropriate duties, customs could expect to be rewarded with additional staffing. In recent years this old model of the way things work has been shattered. In today's customs world we see the following:

- Workloads do not increase incrementally, they increase exponentially.
- Budget and staffing do not increase at the level of transactions, and resources may actually decrease.
- Customs is not expected to choose between enforcement and facilitation; they must improve both.

In this regard customs faces many of the same challenges faced by industries competing in the global economy. Japanese companies have demonstrated, for example, that cost and quality can and must be delivered at the same time. Every company and product is now judged on its capacity to deliver on cost, quality, and speed. Industry has developed new tools and techniques to compete in this new environment. Many of these same tools and techniques are applicable to customs and are now being adopted by customs organizations of various sizes and stages of development. These tools include the following:

- automation of the redesigned customs process
- advanced data analysis techniques
- risk management and compliance measurement
- audit and account management approaches
- objective measurement of customs and importers performance
- business solutions such as Business Process Management
- development of strategic alliances with business and other government agencies

Utilization of these approaches is the basis for building a world-class customs organization. As a step in this process, customs must look at its work and think about its workload in an new light. Greater analytical capabilities and the elements of ICMP make this new view of customs work and its workload possible.

Return for a moment to Figure I.1, which defines the goal of customs from the viewpoint of customs and the business community. Simply stated, the goal of customs is compliance with customs laws and reduction in cost and time for both customs and business. We now have the tools to measure our progress toward these goals.

In terms of workload, we must stop thinking about the individual passengers, shipment, or entry as the basic unit of work. We must also stop thinking of the work of customs as "processing" these entries and cargo. Computers and automated systems are now available to do the processing and are much more accurate and reliable at this routine work. Customs employees can now be liberated from the drudgery of routine transaction-by-transaction work and can focus their efforts on major programs and activities which increase compliance, improve enforcement, and facilitate the movement of goods through customs. This work is of a higher level, is more rewarding, and leads to measurable progress toward important national goals. This work entails looking at entire countries, industries, and companies to determine the level of risk they pose and the level of compliance they have achieved.

ANALYZING AND CATEGORIZING CUSTOMS WORK

As we move away from the transaction as the basic unit of work for customs and its employees, we must determine our new unit of work and measurement. To do that, we must again consider our assessment of the environment. What did that assessment reveal to us? Is there a concern in the country about customs revenues or about moving cargo or passengers more quickly through customs? Is there a rising crime rate fueled by trafficking in narcotics, guns, or other contraband? Is transnational crime emerging as one of the major issues of the next century?

For many countries, customs is an important source of revenue for their national government. A goal for customs, therefore, may be to ensure that all appropriate customs duties are collected. Under the traditional customs approach, customs officers would begin scrutinizing every entry and cargo shipment for revenue implications. In many cases this would indeed increase revenues. At the same time it might cause costs to rise for both customs and business and for enforcement and compliance to decrease in other areas.

There is an alternative approach to the work of customs that can produce the appropriate increased revenues without increasing costs or decreasing effectiveness in other enforcement or compliance areas. This alternative is based on an analysis of the data in customs automated systems as well as those obtained from external sources. Data in customs files regarding imported goods are a national resource of great value to business, other government agencies, and customs itself. The value of the data is multiplied when the data are supplemented by information obtained from other government agencies, other customs administrations, and trade data from sources such as the Internet.

As an alternative to scrutinizing every entry for revenue implications, we would look to the database as our first step in addressing the revenue problem. In this case we would do an analysis of major revenue producers. That is, we would examine the data and database to determine which importers account for most of the revenue. At the same time we might look at which commodities and which exporting countries provide most of the revenues. What customs administrations typically determine during this process is that a relatively small number of importers, commodities, exporting countries, and entries account for the vast majority of revenue. A version of the 80–20 rule frequently applies; that is, 20 percent of the importers account for 80 percent of the revenue. This can only be determined through an analysis and categorization of the data.

Once we have made the determination of who these large revenue producers and entities are, we can begin a process to focus on these entities as the target of our revenue project. Along with the focus on specific entries, we can bring to bear other elements of the ICMP process, such as audit, on the revenue improvement initiative. The advantages of this analytical approach to addressing a problem include a focus only on the specific problem area, no disruption to those importers and entries of little or no concern, no negative impact on other compliance and enforcement areas, and a saving of resources to focus on other problem areas.

While the example used here is revenue, the analytical approach to customs problems and opportunities applies equally well to other customs responsibilities, such as quota, country of origin, or classification. Analysis of the database can help customs focus on a specific problem and develop a specific solution without disrupting the entire trade community or involving the entire customs workforce. In the long term, analysis provides the foundation for achieving greater facilitation while increasing compliance and enforcement. To increase both compliance and facilitation at the same time, it will require the application of the remaining elements of ICMP.

Developing these analytical skills is essential for those customs services which hope to keep pace with increases in travel and trade and to eventually move to the top echelon of customs organizations around the world. To make the transition to an analytical, information-driven customs administration, the appropriate investments in hardware, software, and human resources will have to be made. Moving from the transaction-driven, traditional approach used by most customs administrations is a culture change, but the commitment will result in a high payoff if the leadership of the organization perseveres.

Data analysis is a powerful tool in the enforcement area as well. Consider the area of worldwide heroin trafficking by couriers. Several years ago many customs administrations were faced with an epidemic of heroin traffic via body carriers and swallowers. This heroin originated in Southeast Asia, was transported through Africa, was transshipped through Europe, and was destined for the United States. Under the traditional method of operating, customs administrations, presumably on four continents, were addressing the problem. Ironically, under the old paradigm of customs workload and measures, each customs may have viewed their operation as a success as each was interdicting and seizing more heroin and arresting more heroin traffickers. Statistics were impressive. Requests for new staffing and resources may have even been made based on the new workload and heroin threat. To add to the irony, major heroin traffickers were almost certainly as happy. The loss of a small percentage of the heroin and the arrest of an equal percentage of couriers was a cost of doing business. The lost heroin and couriers could be easily replaced from the huge profits of the successful smuggling attempts. This is an example of the revolving door of the international customs and law enforcement system, and how that system is preyed upon by transnational criminal organizations. Fortunately, it is also an example of how customs organizations can cooperate internationally, look at their work differently, employ different measures, and utilize data analysis to resolve a problem rather than deal with its symptoms.

In this case, one or more customs administrations began analyzing their arrest and seizure data and noticed the significant increases in heroin body carriers and swallowers. Further analysis revealed a pattern of airlines and flights preferred by the traffickers. At some point, customs administrations began sharing their data and experiences, culminating in meetings hosted by the WCO to address the problem on a more global basis. The solution was the product of additional data analysis, this time on a global basis and analyzing data available in airline systems as well. While no drug abuse or drug trafficking problem is ever completely eliminated for all time, this is an example of a trafficking problem being severely curtailed as a result of international cooperation based on innovative problem solving supported by national and international data analysis.

VALUE OF CUSTOMS DATA

The value of the data in customs systems goes beyond customs. These data include information on carriers and conveyances, frequency of travel or importation, value, emerging trade patterns, growth industries, and sources of goods, and can be combined with information from carriers and other agencies to enable customs to look beyond the individual trade or travel transaction to examine the practices of entire companies, industries, or countries. These data form the basis for national trade statistics and are used by economists for macroeconomic analysis. They can pinpoint growth and change in industry sectors by analysis of harmonized system numbers. These data can do all of this and more, and also enable customs to identify anomalies that might signal fraud or bribery. Every customs automated system should be developed with these analytical goals in mind.

Customs data are also of great value to other government agencies involved in border activities. Those agencies can use these data to improve their enforcement and compliance levels. Traditional enforcement approaches can achieve just so much compliance. To achieve 100-percent compliance through traditional enforcement methods would not only require resources that governments will not be willing to provide but would entail delays and costs to industry that the public would not permit. Automation, data analysis, BPM, risk management, and compliance measurement provide an alternative approach that will result in unprecedented and previously unattainable levels of compliance and facilitation.

CONCLUSION

Data analysis is a force multiplier. It is a powerful strategic tool for policy makers for deploying resources and establishing priorities to those problems and opportunities that will produce the most significant results. It places in the hands of the individual customs officer information and perspective on customs issues and problems that is international in scope. It helps resolve the old dilemma of not "seeing the forest for the trees," with the trees being the transactions. When combined with automation, data analysis becomes the lever to propel customs to new levels of efficiency and effectiveness in compliance as well as trade facilitation. In the next section and subsequent chapters we will learn how to leverage the enablers of TQM and BPM, automation, and data analysis to employ advanced customs techniques and increase customs effectiveness.

Recommendations from Chapter 6

- Recognize that new automation and information technology tools enable customs to change the way it does business.
- Employ these new tools to require machines to do transaction-by-transaction processing and to liberate employees to higher-level work.
- Concentrate efforts on analysis of enforcement and compliance problems and objectives.
- Use analytical techniques to look at compliance and enforcement problems from the perspective of entire industries, companies, countries, and trading blocs.
- Focus on larger issues of noncompliance and enforcement with the objective of moving closer to 100-percent compliance and resolving major enforcement problems.
- Develop a competency within the organization in data analysis.
- Use new data analysis capabilities to leverage effectiveness in enforcement and to employ new techniques in audit and risk management.
- Incorporate the data analysis, enforcement, and compliance requirements of other government agencies in all customs programs to achieve maximum efficiency and effectiveness of government programs at the border.
- Develop and integrate customs data with data from external sources to improve targeting for enforcement and compliance.

Actions for Global Customs Managers for Chapter 6

The enabling skills and technology of Business Process Management, automation, and data analysis are making it possible for organizations large and small, in government as well as industry, to attain new levels of effectiveness. More and more frequently, information is the ingredient added by organizations to make their products more valuable. Some customs administrations are beginning to demonstrate how using the data in automated customs systems can enable them to look at entire companies, commodities, industries, and countries. By looking at data in this holistic fashion, with the goals of compliance and facilitation in mind, customs can transform its operation from transaction to information driven. By cooperating with customs in the development of process management, information technology and data analysis businesses can increase mutual trust and confidence in their organizations and systems.

The enabling processes are the means by which customs and industry leverage their organizations to new heights of compliance and facilitation. As customs better understands industry systems, the groundwork is laid for fewer time-consuming, intensive, intrusive, and costly inspections. Industry can also provide perspective on worldwide customs performance that can only be garnered by first-hand experience in dealing with every customs service in the world. The data available to individual international carriers and multinational trades have never been gathered, collated, and analyzed with the purpose of providing feedback to customs at the national, regional, and international levels.

The enabling processes of Business Process Management, automation, and data analysis should be a two-way street, with customs providing data to industry to help them become more compliant with customs and other government agency requirements and industry providing feedback on worldwide customs best practices and the implementation of standard worldwide systems and procedures. Analysis of data by businesses provides a number of benefits to both customs and the trade:

- a worldwide snapshot from the industry perspective of best practices by customs around the world
- insight as to customs problem areas in general as well as specific terms
- guidance to customs at the international, regional, and national levels as to improvements that could be made in the international trading system
- an analysis of costs, processing times, and other inefficiencies in the trade process in quantitative terms
- information for other agencies on steps they might take to improve the import and export process
- information on costs and processing times that can be used by companies to make business decisions on locations for trade and investment

Throughout this process, care must be taken to ensure that it is done, and that it is perceived by customs as being done, in a constructive way. In some countries, customs has not developed a relationship of trust and confidence sufficient to endure criticism from industry. In others, the customs reaction could be defensive or, worse, retaliatory. The objective should be to establish a dialogue between government and industry that is based on trust, confidence, shared data, and mutual goals.

NOTE

1. Malcolm K. Sparrow, *Imposing Duties: Government's Changing Approach to Compliance* (Westport, Conn.: Praeger, 1994), 112.

————————————————— PART III

THE ADVANCED
TECHNIQUES

CHAPTER 7

Improve Enforcement

*There is a certain foolishness in traditional enforcement ap-
proaches. They wait until the damage is done and then they react,
case by case, incident by incident, failure by failure. Enforcement
agencies accept the work in the form in which it arrives, and,
therefore have tended to organize their activities around failure
rather than around opportunities for interventions.*

—Malcolm K. Sparrow, *Imposing Duties:
Government's Changing Approach to Compliance*[1]

Enforcement of laws at the nation's borders is a critical component of every customs administration. While every customs administration has an enforcement
element, the authorities, responsibilities, and roles of each customs organization
vary widely. Some customs agencies have vast powers to arrest, search, seize,
and investigate possible violation of customs laws. Others have more limited
powers, focusing on the inspection of goods and the classification and valuation
of merchandise. Each customs service must design its enforcement strategy based
on the authority provided to it under the law. Under ICMP, every customs administration can initiate their enforcement program from the same point of
departure. The starting point for all customs is to achieve 100-percent compliance with all customs laws and other government agency laws at the border. While no customs can achieve 100-percent compliance, the tools of ICMP
enable customs to move closer to that goal and to measure progress toward it.

The importance of customs enforcement is increasing every day as a result
of the rise in transnational crime. In this chapter we will (1) review traditional
approaches to customs law enforcement, (2) identify the need for a threat
assessment, (3) establish the need for enforcement strategies, (4) introduce
an enforcement problem-solving model, and (5) show the relationship between enforcement and other elements of ICMP.

TRADITIONAL CUSTOMS ENFORCEMENT

Until and including modern times, the focal point of customs enforcement
has been the customs inspector and the primary tool has been the customs
inspection. The unit of work for customs has traditionally been the individual
passenger, shipment, and conveyance. The work has been reactive and se-
quential. In recent decades, as travel and trade have increased dramatically
every year, customs has been challenged by a deluge of cargo and travelers,
often resulting in long delays as customs processed its workload transaction
by transaction. For many years customs sought to cope with these increases
in workload with more personnel and larger budgets. In very few cases did
resources keep pace with the exponential increases in traffic at the nation's
borders. Customs morale typically suffered. Customs management often gave
policy makers the difficult choice of selecting either facilitation of travelers

and trade on the one hand or good enforcement of customs laws to prevent smuggling and customs fraud, including revenue fraud, on the other.

Customs is not alone in facing the dilemma of increased demands for both better enforcement and service to the public. Dr. Malcolm K. Sparrow at the John F. Kennedy School at Harvard University has researched the work of police, environmental protection, and tax administration agencies.[2] Sparrow suggests that other compliance and enforcement agencies "confront crushing operations loads which absorb virtually all available resources, and have enforcement strategies which have traditionally relied heavily upon the mechanism of deterrence, fueled through vigorous prosecutorial efforts." He goes on to speculate that "perhaps other enforcement professions, like these three, feel torn between demands for increased service orientation and tougher enforcement? Should they get friendlier or tougher? Perhaps they feel the need for a better understanding of the relationship between compliance production and service provision." Enlightened customs administrations demonstrate that a world-class customs organization can produce both record levels of customs compliance and enforcement and greatly facilitated customs service for travelers and the importing community.

THREAT ASSESSMENT

A good customs enforcement program begins with a threat assessment. Within customs and the customs community there is broad knowledge of the enforcement problems facing customs. An enforcement threat assessment brings together in a formal way all of the available information from all sources about violations of the nation's laws at the borders. To perform the threat assessment, a crossfunctional team of customs officers should be established. This team should include personnel from every discipline. The customs officers should be a representative sample of the geography of the country and include personnel from air, land, and seaports. Veteran officers as well as employers newer to the organization should be included to ensure that new ideas and perspectives are provided. The idea of including personnel from other law enforcement organizations should be explored.

The purpose of the threat assessment is to provide the organization with the best and most concise possible picture and description of the problems of customs and other agency compliance and enforcement at the border. The starting point for the threat assessment is the environmental assessment described in Chapter 1. The threat assessment team should review the data in the environmental assessment pertaining to international and domestic crime problems and use those data as a foundation for data collection on customs and border violations. Crime and violation data from the environmental assessment will be supplemented by data from the following sources:

- information in news reports about domestic and international crime problems

- data from customs' own files on violations, seizures, penalties, arrests, investigations, and related enforcement information
- information from the World Customs Organization on transnational crime and customs violations
- information from other law enforcement organizations that may have a connection with international trade and travel
- attendance at domestic and international law enforcement conferences sponsored by Interpol, the WCO, or other international law enforcement organizations
- data from customs automated systems that might provide insight as to emerging or changing crime patterns and problems
- the results of customs special enforcement operations
- data from customs compliance measurement and risk management systems
- the views of customs employees at every level on customs enforcement problems and issues

Information gathered in the threat assessment should be placed in categories, such as customs fraud, narcotics trafficking, money laundering, and export violations. The data from the threat assessment will be assigned priorities and used as inputs to customs enforcement strategies.

ENFORCEMENT STRATEGIES

Upon completion of the threat assessment, customs will develop strategies to deal with enforcement problems. These enforcement strategies will typically include customs fraud, money laundering, narcotics trafficking, and export violations. The strategies may be broken out by air, land, and sea. Strategies will be further subdivided by type of violation, as in the following examples:

- Customs fraud might include intellectual property rights violations, revenue fraud, transshipment, other agency violations, or false invoicing to avoid quotas or other restrictions.
- Narcotics trafficking might be broken out by heroin, cocaine, marijuana, and dangerous drugs, and cover smuggling at the ports as well as between the ports.
- Money laundering would address physical movement as well as wire transfers, and cover movements by passengers along with cargo concealments.
- Export violations would address all modes of transport and ensure compliance with all laws, with possible emphasis on trafficking in weapons and munitions.

The threat assessment and priorities would be provided to all employees. Once the threat assessment has been completed and the strategies developed, implementation plans must also be developed. The implementation plans would encompass all aspects of the organization and may include changes to customs processes as a means to improve enforcement and compliance by preventing violations. The plans may include public relations and involving the business and trade community in the enforcement process. Each component of the customs organization should be briefed on the strategies and understand their role in implementing them. A key element of each strategy should be the creation of crossfunctional and ad hoc enforcement teams to address and implement various aspects of the enforcement problem and strategy. The effective organization is constantly establishing and disbanding these special teams to generate enthusiasm, involvement, and expertise through broad participation by employees.

Each strategy should identify the problem, establish goals, define roles for the permanent organization, determine necessary changes in process, identify needs for special teams, and include measures of success and evaluation criteria. Enforcement strategies should also be supplemented by an approach to enforcement that utilizes problem-solving techniques.

ENFORCEMENT PROBLEM SOLVING

While ICMP is a powerful tool for achieving customs compliance and improving customs enforcement, it will not automatically resolve all customs enforcement problems. International drug traffickers, money launderers, arms traffickers, and criminals are not candidates for informed compliance and industry partnerships. Specific enforcement programs must be developed to address the most significant customs enforcement programs. It should also be clear that while customs has a significant role in addressing international crime such as narcotics trafficking customs alone cannot succeed to any significant degree. For major international crime programs to have any significant impact, partnerships and coalitions must be developed among customs and domestic police organizations as well as other customs services and the business community. Other government agencies and social organizations must also be brought into the process. In the case of drug abuse, the family, the medical community, and religious organizations must be part of any long-term solution.

The fact that some international customs and crime problems are so complex and massive should not discourage customs from pursuing its enforcement responsibilities. Customs should, however, examine its current enforcement programs in light of powerful international crime organizations and the pressure brought to bear on customs at the border because of increased travel and trade. It should be clear that the traditional transaction-by-transaction approach will not work. Traditional customs enforcement approaches to interdiction, inspection, and investigation must be supplemented by new approaches to increase enforcement effectiveness.

Strategic Problem Solving is a new approach to customs enforcement that incorporates elements of problem-solving policing and community policing that have been very successful in some cities in substantially reducing crime problems. Strategic Problem Solving helps customs officers rethink their traditional view of the enforcement problem and objective. The objective of customs is not to catch smugglers but to prevent and deter smuggling. Obviously, customs must catch some smugglers to stop the criminal activity. For too long, customs has used the number of seizures and arrests and the amount of drugs seized as a measure of enforcement effectiveness. Strategic Problem Solving, with its emphasis on deterrence and prevention, would more likely focus on a particular type of smuggling activity with the objective of eliminating the smuggling problem, significantly reducing the number of occurrences, reducing the severity of the occurrences, or improving the efficiency of processing the violations and the violators. This might actually result in traditional statistics going down rather than up.

Strategic Problem Solving typically utilizes interdisciplinary teams to focus on a specific problem. This team approach is essential, in that it brings different perspectives, points of view, and skills to bear on an enforcement problem. Success can even be greater when customs skills are supplemented with personnel from agencies outside customs which have an interest or stake in the problem as well as skills and authorities that may be brought to bear on it.

The following are the elements of Strategic Problem Solving:

- *Identify the Problem*: Involves data collection, identification of scope and cause, and brainstorming to develop a tentative definition of the enforcement problem.
- *Develop Objectives and Expectations*: Involves determining and stating explicitly the goals and objectives in addressing the problem in measurable terms.
- *Develop and Analyze Alternatives*: Use creative and divergent thinking to assess brainstormed alternatives in terms of the potential of each alternative to reduce, eliminate, or displace the problem.
- *Select Alternatives*: Based on the analysis of the alternatives, select the best alternative or combination of alternatives.
- *Test and Implement*: If time permits or circumstances dictate, alternatives should be tested in advance of implementation. Implementation should be planned in the context of other ongoing customs initiatives.
- *Monitor*: Monitor performance against the established objectives and measures. Determine whether the initiative should be continued, modified, expanded, or canceled.

The following are cases from the files of the U.S. Customs Service that illustrate the Strategic Problem Solving approach to customs enforcement.

OPERATION NOOSE

Problem

The New Orleans area was experiencing a rapid increase in stolen vehicles. In 1994, the area ranked fourteenth in the nation. By 1995, the area jumped to fifth. The National Insurance Crime Bureau (NICB) estimated that 30 percent of the cars were never recovered and that 15 percent were being exported out of the country. The stolen vehicles often command two to three times their value in the overseas market. Theft for profit was one reason for the epidemic, but insurance fraud was also a significant factor. The rings that export stolen vehicles usually have the true identity of the vehicles disguised and use fraudulent documentation. However, many vehicles were not reported stolen at the time of export.

Objective

The objective was to disrupt the flow of stolen vehicles and equipment through the Port of New Orleans and indict, arrest, and prosecute the individuals involved.

Alternatives

Before the customs team began work, they traveled to watch the customs outbound operation in Newark. The Newark operation had been very successful over the years and the New Orleans team wanted to start their operation with Newark's best practices.

The customs team working on this problem then formed a multijurisdictional taskforce with the New Orleans Police Department (NOPD), the Louisiana State Police, and the Harbor Police. They are all co-located in the Customhouse (this came at a time when the NOPD had to disband their auto theft squad because of budget cuts). The team established communication links with the NICB database and designed a standard form that all exporters were required to fill out when exporting a vehicle. The team created a database using the information from their new form to track all exported vehicles. They compared the records of previously exported vehicles in this database with the NICB database to detect cases of insurance fraud and cases where the purchaser never finished paying for the vehicle and it was subsequently reported stolen.

The taskforce had also been developing informants and the port had conducted short-term blitz operations to examine a large number of outbound containers for concealed vehicles. They employed carbon monoxide detectors and hydrocarbon detectors to check a larger number of containers. They increased communication between the document analysis section and the export team, and they conducted a major public relations campaign using both print and electronic media to let people know what they were doing, how they could be contacted, and what kind of information was helpful.

Results

The team began implementing their alternatives on October 1, 1996. Since then, they have seized the following:

64 vehicles

2 snowmobiles

4 trucks

1 tractor trailer

12 weapons

750 rounds of ammunition

28,370 pounds of stolen aluminum

1,170 pounds of stolen copper

They have also arrested fifty-six people connected with the seizures. Two of the cases involved seizures and arrests made at "chop shops" that also had ocean containers on the premises.

The taskforce is still investigating a number of the seizures, and the work of the taskforce is beginning to attract the attention of other agencies and is gaining support within the participating agencies. A Louisiana State Police Major has gone before the Louisiana legislature to obtain additional funding to put more resources into the taskforce.

OPERATION WHITE SHARK

Problem

There was intelligence and anecdotal evidence that smugglers were landing loads of drugs onto the beaches of South Padre Island, Texas, from shark boats. These are open boats that fishermen use to catch sharks in the Gulf of Mexico. However, there had not been any drug seizures from these boats or on the island. The Brownsville Port Director and Resident Agent in Charge (RAC) established a team of customs agents, inspectors, canine officers, and National Guardsmen to work on this problem.

Objective

The first objective was to establish the level of threat, if any, from the shark boats. After the threat level was established, the objective became to disrupt and displace the smuggling operations.

Alternatives

When this operation started in March 1996, only customs agents and inspectors and National Guardsmen were involved. They set up concealed observation stations in the dunes of South Padre Island. They watched the smugglers beach the shark boats, unload the narcotics, and conceal them in the sand dunes. This activity always occurred at night. They would wait, often for many hours, for the domestic smugglers to come to dig up the loads and transport them to the mainland. Rather than arrest the smugglers on the beach and give away their observation sites, they decided to intercept the loads on one of the few causeways that connected the island with the mainland. The observers would radio to other officers when the smugglers were leaving with their loads.

Results

They were wildly successful using these tactics and soon attracted the attention of other law enforcement agencies. Eventually, the Texas Department of Public Safety (DPS), the Coast Guard, the National Park Service, the Cameron County Police, and the Drug Enforcement Administration (DEA) joined the effort.

The smugglers reacted by landing the shark boats short of the mouth of the Rio Grande. They would then smuggle the drugs through Mexico and through the Brownsville port of entry. This was confirmed by some seizures customs and Border Patrol made wherein the drug packages had wet sand on them.

The taskforce notified the Mexican government about the change in the smugglers pattern, and the Mexican Army was dispatched to the beaches below Matamoros. This prevented the smugglers from using that route any longer. They have shifted back to new areas of Padre Island. Some smugglers are traveling as far north as the Corpus Christi area and some come up the mouth of the Rio Grande.

During the time when the RAC and Brownsville were running this operation, they seized in excess of 30,000 pounds of marijuana and cocaine. Recently, the Coast Guard announced a major initiative in the area, called Gulf Shield. They are diverting resources to the western Gulf of Mexico to deny the smugglers access to the Texas coast. The National Park Service was considering sending their trainee officers to Padre Island on temporary duty to also deny the use of the Padre Island National Seashore to the smugglers. These efforts have all evolved out of the project started by the RAC and Port Director for Brownsville.

SOUTH FLORIDA SEAPORT
INTERNAL CONSPIRACIES

Problem

Internal conspiracies at the Miami and Port Everglades seaports were responsible for importing and or controlling thousands of pounds of cocaine and marijuana each year. The Miami Office of Investigations and Field Operations formed a Strategic Problem Solving team to address this issue in February 1996.

Objective

Through the initiation of several enforcement methods, the team sought to keep the longshoremen off balance and remove their sense of security. They also intended to increase the number and volume of narcotics seized at both Miami and Port Everglades seaports. They sought to force the smuggling organizations to utilize methods which could be targeted via data systems.

Alternatives

The team encouraged carriers to install closed-circuit television systems to monitor container yards and vessel off-loading areas, and conducted vehicle stops and searches at various times of the day and night of all vehicles leaving Dodge Island or Port Everglades. The team also used the Miami Contraband Enforcement Team inspectors, agents, Canine Enforcement Officers, and National Guard resources to augment the Port Everglades unit to conduct examinations of cargo as it was unloaded from the vessels. In addition, the team conducted sweeps of the container yards during off hours of operation, conducted overt and covert surveillance of vessel offloads, utilized covert camera systems to identify internal conspirators in the act of accessing narcotics to aid in prosecutions, and aggressively pursued the development of new sources of information and continued to creatively utilize confidential sources, cooperating defendants, and information developed by other law enforcement agencies to infiltrate the various cells of the longshoremen.

Results

Since the beginning of fiscal 1996, the Miami team has seized 10,068 pounds of cocaine in twenty separate seizures. The team has also seized, since October 1, 1996, 3,097 pounds of marijuana in six separate seizures. Of the total of twenty-six seizures, twelve have involved internal conspiracies.

The Strategic Problem Solving methodology described can be an important new tool in the customs arsenal against customs violators and transnational crime. Strategic Problem Solving supplements traditional enforcement operations. Strategic Problem Solving teams are drawn from customs operating personnel and include inspectors, commodity specialists, investigators, analysts, and computer scientists. These teams supplement the vital enforcement operations of all customs personnel in their day-to-day performance. Strategic Problem Solving does not replace, but rather enhances customs investigations, inspections, patrols, special enforcement operations, and periodic intensive focused reviews. If applied systematically to appropriate problems, this process has the potential to produce significant enforcement results.

ICMP AND ENFORCEMENT

Enforcement is not an isolated element of ICMP. Enforcement problems are resolved and compliance is increased when all elements of ICMP are designed and managed with enforcement and compliance in mind. The following sections describe several elements of ICMP aimed at improving customs enforcement.

Assess the Environment

Enforcement begins with the customs environmental assessment. When customs officials begin examining the external world, an examination of international and domestic crime is an integral part of the process. On the international front, customs administrations examine trends in international crime such as narcotics trafficking, money laundering, trafficking in contraband, including weapons and munitions, as well as traditional customs fraud. Customs examines these trends and exchanges information with other customs administrations, the WCO, and other international enforcement agencies to obtain the necessary information and intelligence to develop its strategies to impact, prevent, and deter violations of these types at their borders.

Domestically, customs examines national trends and statistics on crime to determine if there is a link between the domestic crime problem and customs responsibilities at the border, as in the following examples:

- an outbreak of violent crime fueled by illegal trafficking in smuggled firearms, weapons, and ammunition
- crime and violence associated with a drug abuse problem that is caused by the smuggling of narcotics through customs
- illegal money laundering across international borders to disguise the proceeds of illicit activities
- trafficking in counterfeit goods; intellectual property rights violations; or unsafe, unhealthy, or environmentally threatening products smuggled through customs

In assessing the external environment, customs must examine these problems and determine relative priority for enforcement based on danger to the public, significance of the problem, and customs' ability to impact the problem.

Maintain Integrity

Customs plays a major role in national and international enforcement. The need for absolute integrity of the organization and its employees is paramount if the enforcement mission of customs is to be successful. Yet the temptations for corruption caused by the massive amounts of drugs and illicit money and other contraband seized by customs is greater than in any other agency. At the 1996 APEC conference in Manila, the Speaker of the House and the Commissioner of Customs of the Philippines spoke out forcefully and candidly about corruption and the need to ruthlessly attack corruption in customs. Every customs service must adopt and maintain for all time this vigilance against corruption for enforcement or any other program in customs to be successful.

Improve Quality and Manage Processes

Business Process Management is a proven business technique for improving the cost, speed, and quality of business processes from end to end. Some customs administrations are now adopting business management and quality improvement processes. Examples of customs processes are the import process and the passenger process. Management and internal controls must be built into these processes to prevent fraud and abuse on the part of business or employees. These controls enhance the enforcement functions of customs. Enforcement personnel must understand customs operational processes and use and modify them to prevent and deter violations.

Business Process Management accompanied by automation of processes also increases efficiency resulting in greater productivity. Resources saved by Business Process Management and automation can be redirected to higher-level, more rewarding work in enforcement and compliance.

Automating Customs Processes

Automation is absolutely essential to the enforcement element of ICMP. Automation provides the ability to attack significant enforcement problems in several ways:

- Automation saves personnel resources that would otherwise be involved in routine processing of cargo or passengers. As customs officers are relieved of mundane processing responsibilities taken over by computers, the customs personnel are now available for higher-level work in enforcement and compliance.
- Automation provides the platform for analyzing the data in one of customs most important resources, its own database.
- Automation provides the platform for targeting suspect shipments and travelers based on past violations, intelligence, source-country profiles, travel patterns, suspect commodities, and a variety of other criteria.
- Automation provides the ability to receive and process information in advance and select suspect shipments, conveyances, and travelers for extra security.

Automation of customs processes can provide immediate benefits to customs enforcement. As customs gains experience with automation, it is possible to develop extremely sophisticated artificial intelligence programs to support customs enforcement and compliance programs.

Analyze Import and Travel Data

Computerized customs systems provide the opportunity for customs to analyze data in customs databases to detect potential violations and violators. These same analytical capabilities can be used to identify travel and import practices that are suspect. Analysts can also obtain data from other agencies, international trade organizations, and industry to improve the targeting process. Equally important for enforcement purposes, the analytical and computer capability can identify the major importers, which account for the largest amount of goods and most significant revenue, for special attention. As those importers are identified and their compliance is assured, resources normally devoted to them can be partially diverted to other, higher-risk importers. Analysts with special computer skills will be a new category of customs employee necessary to fully realize the benefits of the analytical process.

Informed Compliance and Industry Partnerships

The theory of informed compliance is that the majority of importers will comply with customs requirements when those requirements are stated and presented explicitly and clearly. The stage beyond informed compliance is enforced compliance. Here again, when the concept of informed compliance works in regard to a substantial number of importers more attention can be focused on businesses, organizations, and issues that are suspected violators.

The concept of industry partnership is that industry will frequently assist government in efforts to attack criminal violations such as narcotics trafficking. With the support and leadership of the WCO, several countries have developed partnerships through memoranda of understanding with international air and sea carriers who are determined to ensure that their conveyances are drug free. Engaging the business community and the public in combating drug trafficking, money laundering, and other crimes can result in powerful alliances and add a new dimension to addressing criminal problems. Similar coalitions between government and industry have been developed to address other customs enforcement problems, such as intellectual property rights violations.

At a narcotics conference in Asia several years ago, a Commissioner of Hong Kong Customs stated that it was the policy of Hong Kong Customs to cooperate with any organization devoted to fighting the problem of drug trafficking. That statement inspired the conferees at the time and remains to this day good advice for customs in terms of its relationship with industry, the public, and other government organizations concerned about significant crime problems.

Measure Compliance and Manage Risk

Compliance measurement and risk management are additional tools which can complement the enforcement process. Measurement and risk management are techniques commonly used in business but only recently applied to customs. Introducing these skills in customs management can increase enforcement effectiveness. Skills in measurement can provide insights as to which enforcement programs are working and progress toward achieving enforcement and compliance results. This, in turn, inspires personnel to make additional progress. Risk management techniques apply statistics to pinpoint areas needing attention and areas where compliance is at high levels.

This summary of the role of the various ICMP elements in customs enforcement illustrates the power that ICMP brings to bear on the entire enforcement and compliance issue.

SUMMARY

Enforcement is not the sole province of any one section of customs or any one type of customs employee. ICMP is a process that has as its objective increasingly higher levels of compliance and enforcement effectiveness. It does not leave things to chance. Rather, it is a systematic approach that moves relentlessly to higher levels of compliance and enforcement effectiveness.

Advanced information provided by carriers and importers, automation and the extensive databases developed on customs transactions, and an ability to analyze the information in its automated systems gives customs officers enforcement capabilities never before possible. The problem-solving enforcement techniques described in this chapter are just a few examples of customs' increased capacity to address enforcement problems. Whereas in the past customs officers confronted enforcement problems one by one, new information technology and analysis capabilities enable customs officers to identify larger enforcement problems which, when resolved, will result in a greater impact on compliance. Customs officers, working in teams that include inspectors, investigators, commodity specialists, and analysts, can analyze data files and identify possible enforcement problems by company, industry, or country. Conversely, officers with informant- or case-specific information can develop substantial additional information by manipulation of those same data files. In either case, the results can be astounding.

The problem-solving approach will not replace the vigilance and intuition of the customs inspector, substitute for the customs interdiction team, or do away with the need for an expert cadre of customs investigators. But enforcement problem-solving and data analysis techniques will supplement all traditional enforcement methods and render obsolete and ineffective enforcement approaches that are not supported by advanced data and analysis.

When traditional customs enforcement programs of inspection, interdiction, and investigation are enhanced by ICMP and supplemented by strategic problem solving, customs can achieve substantially higher compliance and greater enforcement results. Involving other law enforcement agencies, industry, and the public can result in even greater success. The importance of customs enforcement is increasing daily as a result of the rise of transnational crime and transnational criminal organizations. Customs must coordinate its enforcement efforts with those of other customs organizations to develop an international customs enforcement network against transnational crime. The WCO should take the lead in this effort, as well as leadership in obtaining the support of the international trade community against transnational crimes of terrorism, cargo theft, child pornography, intellectual property rights violations, narcotics and contraband trafficking, money laundering, and customs fraud.

Recommendations from Chapter 7

- Capitalize on productivity savings made possible by automation and other technology and convert positions from routine processing to enforcement and problem solving.
- Make analyses to define problems of noncompliance, and employ problem-solving techniques to eliminate problems, reduce the number and severity of occurrences, or to increase efficiency in processing.
- Be alert to national and international crime problems that have border connections.
- Establish relationships with domestic police agencies and other customs to form alliances against transnational crime.
- Perform a threat assessment that addresses and prioritizes the major areas of customs violations.
- Based on the threat assessment, develop enforcement strategies to address the major customs enforcement problems (e.g, customs fraud, narcotics trafficking, money laundering, and export violations).
- Use the WCO as a focal point for cooperation and strategies against the transnational crime problems of narcotics trafficking, money laundering, terrorism, child pornography, customs fraud, and intellectual property violations.
- Use individual seizures of significance to support domestic and international enforcement efforts and as a means to identify and eventually dismantle major criminal organizations.
- Enlist industry support in efforts to make all shipments and conveyances free of any taint of crime or contraband.
- Work toward the interface of international customs systems to exchange information on customs violators and violations and transnational crime.

Actions for Global Customs Managers for Chapter 7

Until recently, law enforcement at the border has generally been thought of as almost exclusively the domain of the government. Of all the elements of ICMP, enforcement is most identified as the specific responsibility of customs. In recent years, however, the general public, community organizations, and businesses have recognized that establishing and maintaining public safety, security, and freedom from fear require support and participation by all segments of society. The foundation for community-oriented policing and problem-solving policing—two recent and very successful innovations in law enforcement—are based and dependent upon wide participation in improving the quality of life and ensuring public safety.

When the business community cooperates with law enforcement, the outcome is more likely to result in crime prevention and reduction rather than reactive arrest and punishment after the fact. Examples of business involvement in enforcement and crime prevention include banking and finance, in which financial institutions cooperate with law enforcement agencies to prevent corruption of the international banking system by drug traffickers and money launderers. Cooperation extends to airlines, which have a huge stake in preventing terrorist attacks, hijackings, and bombings on commercial airlines. In Colombia, legitimate manufacturers and exporters and the transportation industry are cooperating and spending substantial sums of money to ensure that narcotics traffickers do not use their merchandise or conveyances to transport drugs or money. The international business community also has a major incentive to prevent cargo theft, another multibillion-dollar criminal activity. Good corporate citizens have established the Business Anti-Smuggling Coalition (BASC), which is designed to ensure the integrity of international cargo shipments from the point of manufacture to the point of retail sale. These are examples of what can and is being done through cooperation between law enforcement officials and the international trade community.

With the rise in transnational crime, the billions of dollars in illicit profits of international crime organizations, and the threat that these organizations pose to governments and society, it is essential that law enforcement officials and business cooperate in combating this menace. Once again, the express courier industry provides examples and models for the application of technology and controls that would be of value for other members of the international trade community. The WCO's Memorandum of Understanding program is another program that should be expanded. The following are suggestions for global trade partners in addressing the transnational crime problem:

- Cooperate with customs and other law enforcement agencies to protect the international trade systems from corruption by criminals.
- Review internal procedures from end to end to determine vulnerability to penetration or use by the criminal element.
- Institute procedures and internal controls to ensure that employees are honest and that systems are secure.
- Provide information to customs on any suspicious circumstances.
- Participate in programs such as the BASC and urge the participation of your colleagues in the business community.
- Invest in systems and technology to ensure the security and integrity of cargo and conveyances in international trade.

The rewards for active participation with customs in protecting the security and integrity of the international trade system are substantial. Passengers are made safe from the threat of international terrorism. Importers and exporters are protected from losses due to cargo theft. Nations are shielded from trafficking in contraband, weapons, narcotics, and money laundering and their consequences. Losses to industry due to theft and pilferage will be reduced. The potential for trade-community support, leadership, and creativity is great, but not yet realized. Finally, cooperation with customs in law enforcement, security, and crime prevention will protect the health, security, and safety of society and the families and children of our nations.

NOTES

1. Malcolm K. Sparrow, *Imposing Duties: Government's Changing Approach to Compliance* (Westport, Conn.: Praeger, 1994), 33.
2. Ibid., x.

CHAPTER 8

Informed Compliance

*Through the campaign for informed compliance enterprises are
expected to be conscious of trading legally.*
— Mr. Duanmu Jun, Deputy Director General,
China Customs General Administration[1]

In almost every country in the world, customs has a history as long and proud
as the country itself. Customs is typically characterized by images of an organization that protects its nation's borders as the first line of defense against
trafficking in narcotics and other contraband, of collectors of revenue, or of
protectors of domestic industry. Organizations which view themselves as successful are the hardest to change. As a major source of revenue in many countries, customs is held in high esteem by senior government officials and a
grateful public. Customs' long history, protectionist roots, and often conflicting pressures from multiple constituencies can make change difficult.

In the new global economy, duty rates are declining and customs is becoming a less significant source of revenue. Transnational crime, such as money
laundering, narcotics trafficking, arms dealing, environmental violations, and
terrorism are increasing at alarming rates. At the same time, global trade,
travel, and investment are becoming more significant factors in a nation's
future growth and prosperity. In this environment, it is appropriate for the
customs organization to examine its role in serving the nation and its approaches to dealing with other organizations in government and in industry.

As a result of its history as a protectionist organization and a barrier to
trade, customs' relationship with the international trade community has often
been acrimonious and adversarial. As a powerful representative of the government at the borders, customs could often exercise its authority in arbitrary
and unpredictable ways. Customs frequently did not feel obliged to provide
notice of changes in policy or procedures or to justify the changes. If these
changes were costly, time consuming, or inconvenient for trade and importers, customs could still count on support for its actions from domestic industry and its allies in government and the public. The new emphasis on
international trade is forcing customs to rethink its approaches for dealing
with the trade community. In some countries, customs is viewing itself as a
"supplier," not only to other government agencies but to industry as well.
Increasingly, those involved in international trade are rethinking their responsibilities for compliance and for supporting customs and other law enforcement agencies in the battle against transnational crime and international
criminal cartels. In this chapter, we discuss (1) informed compliance, (2) industry partnership, and (3) enforcement and industry.

INFORMED COMPLIANCE

"Informed compliance" is the term used to describe a different way of thinking about and interacting with the trade community by customs. Informed

compliance looks upon the import process as a shared responsibility between the commercial entity on the one hand (e.g., carrier, broker, importer, exporter, etc.) and customs on the other. Customs responsibility in this relationship is to inform the trade and industry of its responsibilities in meeting statutory and regulatory requirements for the importation of merchandise and for the control of carriers engaged in international trade. The theory is that the vast majority of importers and carriers and other players want to comply or recognize it is in their best interests to comply with all customs and government requirements. Express courier companies and the advent of just-in-time manufacturing systems are examples of new transportation and industrial practices that encourage industry to work cooperatively with government agencies to ensure they are in compliance with all government requirements so that they can receive the highest possible assurance that the vast majority of their shipments will not be delayed in customs.

For the vast majority that is motivated to comply with customs requirements, it is in the best interest of the government to inform them of all government requirements. This information may be disseminated by a variety of means, including the following:

- publication of all customs laws, regulations, and procedures
- seminars open to all members of the trade community or geared to a specific segment, product, or industry
- electronic bulletin boards and e-mail in advance of proposed changes
- requests for comments in advance of changing a system, procedure, or regulation
- publication of notices of change or new requirements in widely disseminated government bulletins
- periodic "town-hall" meetings to discuss issues, relationships, and processes
- advance binding rulings prior to importation
- compliance assessments which review the entire import process from end to end and result in compliance improvement plans

Informed compliance, as described, helps customs move toward its goal of 100-percent compliance by developing a cooperative relationship with that large portion of the trade community motivated to cooperate and comply. The power and authority of the government can inspire an additional segment of industry to move toward greater compliance. As for the remainder—the deliberate violators—the government now has more time to devote to identifying them, investigating their violations, and taking appropriate enforcement action.

If the government's responsibility under the shared responsibility concept is informed compliance, industry's responsibility is reasonable care. "Reasonable care" is the term used to describe industry responsibility to familiarize itself with customs requirements and to comply with customs laws and regulations as communicated by customs utilizing the various media under the informed compliance approach. Industry's reasonable care responsibility may be partially satisfied by employing a responsible broker, attorney, or consultant to supplement their own knowledge and assist not only with import transactions but with developing importer compliance assessment plans.

Many multinational companies are devoting more time to international customs issues. These companies realize there are benefits to be achieved by greater attention to customs matters on a global basis. Not only can companies avoid penalties and delays in customs processing, but by paying greater attention to customs they can be assured they are taking advantage of preferential customs and trade programs that can reduce duties and taxes. Informed international traders exercise their customs responsibilities by performing self-audits, utilizing outside audit firms or consultants to review their systems and practices, and ensuring that all parts of the organization (i.e., tax, transportation, manufacturing, research and development, and finance) are aware of the corporate responsibilities for international customs compliance. This 360-degree approach to customs compliance will ensure that the company does not run afoul of international laws on labor, trade, intellectual property, environment, health, or agriculture and that it does take advantage of all trade preference programs.

In summary, shared responsibility, informed compliance, and reasonable care are concepts that help customs and the trade community achieve their mutual goals of improving customs compliance and reducing the costs of compliance.

INDUSTRY PARTNERSHIP

Most organizations in government, as well as business, recognize the necessity of improving cooperation, coordination, and communication, internally as well as externally. Organization management and leadership are often frustrated by problems that are characterized as misunderstandings or "failure to communicate." In a world in which the pace of change is increasing rapidly and in an era of high-speed telecommunications and transportation, it is essential that organizations understand their place in the world and their position with respect to other players with whom they interact. For customs administrations in particular, it is important to think through the various organizations with which customs interacts and the nature and purpose of these relationships.

There is an emerging role for customs as a supplier. Customs is a supplier of general and specific information on trade practices and transactions to industry, other government agencies, and other customs services. Customs in the future may be the supplier of export information that initiates the import process in another country.

In industry, a great deal has been written about developing partnerships with suppliers and customers and improving service to customers beyond the customers' expectations. Some customs administrations have moved aggressively in adopting the partnership/customer concept in regard to their dealings with the trade community. Others are more cautious, and some are opposed to the idea of such a relationship.

The source of this caution may be based on experience, tradition, or culture. In terms of experience, it may be that a relationship with importers was "too close" and may have resulted in special treatment for a particular importer or even bribery and corruption. In terms of tradition, it may be that there has been a history of an arm's-length relationship between the trade community and customs. In terms of culture, it may be that some countries emphasize an authoritarian approach by government agencies in dealing with the public and industry.

These are points that must be taken into consideration when examining customs' relationship with industry. Organizational relationships are complex and changes in these relationships can have both positive and negative consequences. We must also take into consideration the context in which potential changes are made in dealings with the public. ICMP provides a framework or context for examining these possible changes in organizational relationships. For example, when ICMP is fully implemented, substantial security and integrity controls are built in through internal controls and checks built into the automation, audit, and integrity elements of ICMP. Thus, vulnerability to bribes and corruption is minimized.

New Zealand has long been recognized as one of the world's premier customs organizations. Still, in recent years New Zealand has embarked on a comprehensive customs reform and modernization program resulting in new legislation, a change in name, a review of its mission and goals, and an examination of its relationship to the business community. Now known as the New Zealand Customs Service, it puts an emphasis on "Service." Its reform and modernization program is called "Service with a Capital 'S'." New Zealand is perhaps the customs world's best example of how the complex issue of customs relationship with the business community should be handled. While ranking in the top echelon in enforcement and service to the public, it is also ranked number one in the world in integrity by Transparency International. The New Zealand example illustrates that enforcement, service, and integrity are not incompatible but rather precisely the characteristics that result in a world-class customs service (see Appendix G for a more detailed examination of New Zealand's modernization success).

A recent book titled *Co-opetition* by Brandenburger and Nalebuff provides a useful guide for organizations examining their external relationships.[2] *Co-opetition* recognizes not only the complexity of interorganizational relationships but also the opportunities provided by rethinking traditional interactions among competing and cooperating corporations. More specifically, the authors urge organizations to challenge the traditional outlook that other companies can be categorized only as suppliers, customers, or competitors and introduce a model wherein other companies and even competitors can be brought into a network relationship as "complementors," to work cooperatively in a particular situation or market. This new network relationship among companies is referred to as a "Value Net." The authors introduce a schematic map to help companies visualize other organizations, relationships, and dependencies, as shown in Figure 8.1.

The new term *complementor* is introduced to describe those companies or organizations which provide a product that will enhance the value of the company's own product. In the automobile industry, companies which add value to automobile manufacturers include oil companies, gas stations, insurance companies, finance companies, and banks, as well as tire and auto parts companies. Each of these companies provide a product which enhances the value of an automobile by making it more accessible and convenient to own or operate.

In the Value Net, the role of a company can change depending on the issue under consideration. In the automobile industry, other car manufacturers will ordinarily be a competitor, but when the government is building roads, the industry cooperates to encourage government to build more roads sooner. Thus, the automobile manufacturers in this instance are complementors to each other. Even in industries characterized by fierce competition, the companies frequently form associations to pursue goals that are common to the entire industry or to lobby government for actions or legislation that would benefit the entire industry.

The role of government agencies and customs and the organizations with which customs interacts is equally if not more complex than the private sectors. You are encouraged to draw your own Value Net with customs at the center. In your customs Value Net, where would you place other government agencies? Brokers? Importers? Exporters? The public? Legislative bodies? Other customs administrations around the world? Warehouse operators? Surety companies? Financial institutions? Contractors? Zone operators? Port authorities? Could you envision that one or more of these entities could occupy more than one position, depending on the issue? Is it possible that in different circumstances a foreign customs administration could be in any one of the four roles as customer, complementor, supplier, or even competitor? If the words customer or partner are still troubling in terms of describing a relationship with the importing community, try "consumers" or "users." In any case, the point to be made is that the roles and relationships are multiple and changing.

On the assumption that legitimate businesses are as opposed to drug trafficking as are government officials, the World Customs Organization has endorsed a program of partnerships with international carriers designed to make it more difficult to carry illicit drugs on international conveyances. This is an instance of a business entity acting as a complementor to a government program to prevent international narcotics trafficking. Cooperation between customs and industry to establish an automated customs system for the processing of imported goods is another example of industry as complementors of a government initiative.

Figure 8.1
The Value Net

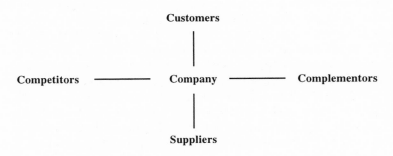

In all instances, however, a state maintains its sovereign authority to enforce and regulate. These various, complex, and changing roles and relationships are admittedly difficult and pose a challenge as well as a danger that the relationships could be abused and lead to corruption. However, with the built-in controls and checks, these risks are minimized and the benefits far outweigh the dangers.

INDUSTRY AND ENFORCEMENT

As world trade has increased and as countries and companies have turned to international trade to increase profits and prosperity, so too have criminal organizations increased their transnational activities. Transnational criminal trafficking in weapons, munitions, and drugs is familiar to all customs organizations. Today, transnational criminal organizations are adding money laundering, fraud, child pornography, environmental crimes, and terrorism to the list of traditional customs violations. Customs alone cannot bring these criminal organizations to justice or stop the trafficking in these illicit industries. Many customs organizations are learning that enlightened and responsible industries share their interest in combating these crimes and organizations. Multinational companies do not want their good names besmirched by any association with international organized crime and international carriers can be as concerned with utilization of their aircraft and vessels by organized crime. Acting in concert with importers and carriers, customs has the potential to do a better job in keeping shipments and conveyances free from any taint of illicit substances. The WCO is encouraging such alliances. These industry and customs partnerships are only in their infant stages but have the potential to increase customs enforcement effectiveness and improve the quality of life around the world.

CONCLUSION

The interests of customs and the legitimate international trade community coincide. Both are committed to ensuring compliance with customs laws, to reducing the cost of compliance, and to facilitating complying goods. New tools in information technology and data analysis combined with new business techniques and approaches enable customs and industry to cooperate to achieve their shared objectives. While customs retains its sovereign responsibilities and can resort to enforcement measures if companies violate the laws, a cooperative and collaborative approach will work best with most responsible companies and industries. Customs and industry should now turn to the employment of cooperative approaches to combating transnational crime.

Recommendations from Chapter 8

- Take advantage of ICMP information and techniques to transform your relationship with legitimate industry.
- Provide industry with all information required for them to achieve compliance with customs and other agency laws (e.g., tariffs, regulations, rulings, procedures, change notices, processes, and appeals).
- Recognize the emerging role of customs as a supplier to industry, other government organizations, and other customs administrations.
- Provide industry with information on their compliance level and help them develop plans to improve compliance.
- Encourage customs brokers and consultants to provide industry full-service assistance in developing and implementing compliance improvement plans.
- Employ progressive sanctions when industry fails to comply and in those instances where deliberate noncompliance is discovered.
- Reduce inspections on high-compliance importers and redirect attention and resources on low-compliance importers and deliberate violators.
- Work with industry, importers, and carriers to ensure that all shipments are free of contraband and secure from terrorists and cargo theft.

Actions for Global Customs Managers for Chapter 8

The increase in the volume of international trade and a recognition of the importance of international trade, travel, and tourism to the development of national economies is creating new opportunities for cooperation between customs and industry and for improving the relationships and processes to facilitate commerce. Customs administrations are coming to realize that there are better ways to deal with the huge increases in travel and trade than the traditional transaction-by-transaction, entry-by-entry, and passenger-by-passenger formulas of the past. Customs authorities are also realizing that the vast majority of companies and passengers are legitimate and law abiding and willingly comply with government requirements. The WCO is encouraging this evolution in customs thinking worldwide and has made customs reform and modernization its flagship program. The WCO is providing the leadership to bring together the World Trade Organization, the United Nations Conference on Trade and Development, the International Chamber of Commerce, and international financial institutions to encourage this reform and modernization. These changes in attitude and approach of customs at the international, regional, and national levels provide industry an unprecedented opportunity to participate in the reform and modernization of the international trading systems. The following are suggested actions for industry in developing a cooperative relationship with customs:

- Engage with customs at the international, regional, and national levels to improve the international trading system.
- Encourage customs reform and modernization at the highest levels of government to provide the political will necessary to foster long-term commitment to reform and modernization.
- Fully use brokers, consultants, and other trade experts in developing compliance plans.
- Join and participate in national and international trade organizations active in improving the trade system.
- Participate in customs seminars and meetings to build relationships as well as expertise.
- Offer to participate in programs to improve customs performance, such as the WCO cycle-time measurement program.
- Cooperate with customs in enforcement programs, such as BASC, to prevent illegitimate free riders on the international system of free trade.

The actions outlined are not just steps to improve relationships or establish partnerships as ends in themselves. These actions help build mutual trust and confidence based on shared information and provide the foundation for achieving the goals of higher compliance, faster release times, and lower costs.

NOTES

1. Duanmu Jun, Speech, Asia–Pacific Economic Cooperation Conference, Manila, October 18, 1996.

2. Adam Brandenburger and Barry Nalebuff, *Co-opetition* (New York: Doubleday, 1996), 17, 23.

CHAPTER 9

Audit

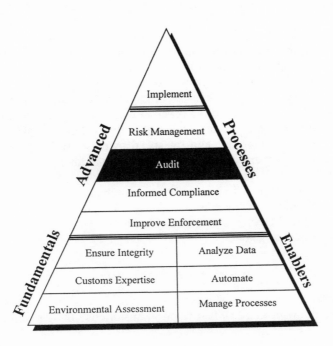

*Although the technological capabilities for creating tomorrow's
organization already exist, nevertheless, I expect that it will take
decades actually to mature because protectionist staffs will resist
internal pressures for greater efficiency, just as protectionist tariffs resist external pressures.*

—Stan Davis, *Future Perfect*[1]

In Part I, we focused on strengthening customs as an institution by exploring
the future in which customs will operate, increasing customs expertise and
developing institutional knowledge, and creating an environment of integrity.
In Part II, we learned of the powerful tools of Business Process Management,
information technology, and data analysis that can put information into the
hands of customs and that the customs officer can use to leverage customs to
new levels of effectiveness. In Part III, we have so far demonstrated the applications of these tools in the area of enforcement and dealings with the private
sector. Building on all these capabilities, it is now appropriate to consider a
change in customs practice that can substantially increase customs effectiveness and reduce the cost of customs to both the industry and government.

The techniques of audit and account management are a significant departure from traditional customs practices in many countries. As discussed in
Chapters 6 and 8, the traditional approach to customs processing is transaction by transaction, shipment by shipment, or passenger by passenger. As
cargo arrives by air, sea, or land, entries are presented to customs. Customs
officers make determinations on inspection and admissibility, classify and
appraise the goods, collect appropriate revenue and statistics, and enter the
goods for consumption, warehouse, or transit.

Depending on the skills, integrity, and training of the officers, the volume
of trade, the complexity of the transactions, and the amount of time available,
this traditional system of customs processing can result in both substantial
compliance and adequate service. However, as the volume of trade, the complexity of issues, and the demand for speed increase in comparison to the
available resources, there will be a predictable breakdown that may be characterized by loss of revenue, slow processing, backlogs, low employee morale, breaches of integrity, failure to detect contraband, or all of these results.
Audit and account management provide an approach for dealing with increasing volumes of trade while at the same time increasing compliance with customs and other agency laws.

THE CUSTOMS AUDIT

Only in recent decades have customs administrations begun to introduce
audit as one of the primary skills and programs of customs. The introduction

of a professional audit program provides a multitude of benefits to customs, including the following:

- the ability to look at an importer's activity as an integrated whole rather than on a transaction basis
- the ability to select particular importers for audit attention based on risk, volume, or other factors
- the ability to focus on importers who represent a significant revenue source (this is particularly important for developing countries for whom customs collections account for a large percentage of government revenues)
- an important internal control and independent integrity check to ensure that appropriate revenues have been collected

Audit is a profession. It must be systematically introduced into the organization as part of the long-term modernization process. As experience is gained with audit, it becomes a more integral, powerful, and sophisticated tool. At first, application of the audit process is typically to protect and increase revenues. Audit is one of the tools that can help customs replace preshipment inspection companies. In the longer term, audit provides a capacity for achieving compliance with other government requirements.

The concept of customs audit can be related to Japanese industrial concepts of quality. Instead of relying on expensive quality inspection programs to look at each manufactured item from the assembly line, the Japanese developed quality programs that built quality in and applied statistical techniques to ensure product quality. The International Standards Organization (ISO) utilizes this same approach in certifying systems as capable and proven approaches for delivering products of a uniform high quality.

The concept of audit in customs is similar. The idea of the customs audit is to determine if the importer has developed an internal system to produce customs entries that are in compliance with customs laws. If that importer's system is thoroughly reviewed and determined satisfactory to produce customs entries in compliance with requirements pertaining to classification, value, origin, and all other substantive requirements, that system creates an opportunity for customs to break the stranglehold of transaction-by-transaction processing and move toward a systems approach based on audit, quality principles, and scientific statistical sampling. We will call this approach of applying audit, quality principles, and statistical sampling to the customs process the *compliance assessment*. This is part of the evolutionary process of audits.

The compliance assessment is not for every importer. It is applicable to those importers identified through the data analysis process as accounting for a significant number of entries and a significant proportion of customs revenues. By identifying these importers and utilizing the compliance assessment process, the customs service can be assured that the "major players" will be in compliance. Another benefit of the compliance assessment to both customs and industry is that the cargo and entries of companies participating in the compliance assessment process no longer require the intensive transaction-by-transaction scrutiny of the traditional customs processing system. The compliance assessment is of mutual benefit to the government and to the importing community. It is an example of the classic win–win situation. The following summarizes the benefits to government and industry:

Benefit to Customs	Benefit to Industry
results in higher compliance	reduces costs
ensures collection of revenue	facilitates entry
saves resources to redirect to high-risk transactions	results in uniform, reliable, and consistent service
	avoids future penalties and other sanctions

The compliance assessment and audit approach can be enhanced by an electronic funds transfer capability and a surety bond system that can provide additional benefits of ensuring the timely deposit of revenues, reducing the risk of importer fraud, and minimizing opportunities for integrity violations.

The bottom line for industry of the compliance assessment and audit approach is that it makes the country a more desirable and reliable place for business and investment. For customs, compliance assessment and audit mean higher compliance and more resources to attack the significant enforcement and noncompliance problems facing the nation. For example, in one country an audit of a large multinational company revealed an extremely high compliance rate. As a result, the customs administration was able to reduce the approximately five hundred physical inspections per year to less than fifty. The savings to the company in dollars and time were enormous. The savings to customs were of similar magnitude, with the resources being invested in other high-risk enforcement areas. Those achievements are made possible by ICMP and particularly the introduction of information technology, data analysis, and compliance measurement skills.

ACCOUNT MANAGEMENT

The analysis of data that results in compliance assessment and audit as an approach to the work of customs identifies importers as candidates for account management. These importers essentially become accounts of customs. At some point, it becomes desirable to establish account managers for these major players. Account management provides a single point of contact for that importer for all customs matters nationwide. The account management approach complements the audit process and enhances the service aspect of customs. As other nations adopt the audit, compliance assessment, and account management processes, there may be opportunities for the exchange of information among international customs account managers, making the international customs process more sophisticated, seamless, and highly compliant.

The process as described applies to the major players and large importers. However, the techniques of data analysis and categorizing importers by accounts and measuring their compliance is applicable to smaller players as well. This means that similar approaches to achieving compliance for smaller players can be applied at the port or field level as a bottom-up application for achieving compliance. Taken together (i.e., top-down compliance assessment and audit accounts for large players and bottom-up for smaller players), the result is high compliance from top to bottom. In the future, the bottom-up port compliance approach may be deemed the most efficient and effective for achieving compliance. If customs is successful in developing the tools and training its personnel in the techniques of analysis and compliance measurement at the port level, compliance could be substantially increased at a rapid pace.

IMPLEMENTATION OF AUDIT AND ACCOUNT MANAGEMENT

Audit is an important discipline and skill that customs organizations must employ in order to modernize. The ability to add audit to the traditional customs skills in classifying, appraising, determining origin, and inspecting provides a whole new dimension to customs capacity to achieve compliance, while reducing the costs of compliance and facilitating the flow of goods through customs. Audit, compliance assessment, and account management do not replace the traditional customs disciplines. They complement them and enable customs to carry out its function more effectively and efficiently.

The audit approach enables customs to determine that a particular importer has developed the necessary systems to produce entries and other customs documentation that are in compliance with customs and other government agency requirements. By inspecting an appropriate statistical sample of shipments and reviewing in-depth a small sample of documentation customs can ensure that the system is, in fact, producing entries that comply.

Introducing the audit discipline in customs may be done by either a recruitment and staffing process to hire new auditors or a contract basis to employ a firm with proven audit skills. In either case, the responsibility for the integration of the audit discipline with other customs functions remains with customs. The audit team must be trained in or supplemented by personnel with expertise in customs classification, valuation, and other customs-related disciplines.

As with the introduction of any new discipline within an organization, if not handled properly the introduction of audit can be difficult and acrimonious resulting in turf battles and squabbling within the organization. Top management must provide leadership and oversight of the new audit function and provide the perspective of how audit fits into the customs organization and how it will contribute to customs goals and complement other customs skills. Audit can provide immediate and sometimes dramatic results, but a successful audit program will require commitment and perseverance for a number of years to ensure a successful implementation and integration.

The introduction of account management should not be undertaken until all of the elements of ICMP, including audit, have been implemented and mastered at all levels of the organization. When this has been accomplished, it is appropriate to consider an account approach. Account management, like audit, requires the introduction of a new skill and new classification of employee. This employee must have a mastery of customs skills, understand the goals of the organization, and possess a capacity for dealing with the public and representing the organization. In the long term, customs organizations will move toward categorizing all business entities with which it deals as accounts. Customs will employ all of the elements of ICMP to raise the compliance level of all businesses and to reduce the costs to government and industry. In this sense, audit and account management represent the future of customs.

CONCLUSION

Audit and account management are advanced techniques that build on the fundamental skills of customs and the enablers of automation, information technology, Business Process Management, and data analysis. Audit provides a powerful internal control to protect customs integrity. For developing countries, audit can be used as a tool to ensure that proper revenues are being collected. More advanced customs administrations can introduce compliance assessment and account management techniques. For those customs administrations determined to regain their autonomy from preshipment inspection, audit should be a consideration in their long-term plan.

Recommendations from Chapter 9

- Develop a competency in customs audit and compliance assessment.
- Audit importers and other customs entities to determine their compliance rates.
- Assess importers and other customs entities to determine whether their customs systems are producing information that will result in compliance with customs and other agency laws.
- Reduce inspections on importers who achieve high levels of compliance and whose systems produce information that results in compliance.
- Select for audit those importers with the largest entry volumes and those dealing with the highest risk and most sensitive commodities. Developing countries should address those companies and industries with the largest potential for revenue collection.

- Consider movement to national account management to provide oversight and service to major importers.
- Develop a capacity for virtual account management for all importers, to be implemented at the port level.

Actions for Global Customs Managers for Chapter 9

Just when international traders were becoming comfortable with the idea of post-audit, customs administrations in some parts of the world started experimenting with pre-audit. But the concepts of audit, pre or post, and compliance assessment are the same. They are concepts derived from industry itself (e.g., ISO 9000). The idea of audit and compliance assessment is to determine whether the importer (or other industry partner regularly providing data to customs) has developed systems and controls (particularly automated systems) that produce information on customs activity that meets all of customs' requirements. If the industry partner has such systems and has developed and maintained a good track record with customs, the expectation is that inspection, document reviews, and other intrusive, costly, and time-consuming interventions by customs will be minimized. As audit-type approaches become the standard around the world, the savings potential for industry is in the billions on an annual basis. At the same time, the potential for just-in-time manufacturing and worldwide integrated logistics systems can be more fully realized when the potential for delays at customs is minimized. To realize these benefits, of course, industry must be willing to provide customs the data it needs and subject their systems to the intense scrutiny necessary to determine that the system and processes are capable of achieving compliance with customs and other government agency laws.

The concept of account management with customs is still in its embryonic stages. From the industry perspective, the notion of having customs accounts with multiple countries raises some interesting questions. A major importer dealing with a dozen or more major customs as an account would suggest interesting comparisons regarding the efficiency and effectiveness and uniformity of the account concept. These comparison and insights could be helpful to customs in evaluating the concept.

In general, audit and account management should be helpful to both government and industry in meeting the goals of improved compliance, faster cycle time through customs and other government agencies, and reduced costs of compliance. The following actions on the part of international traders should be considered:

- Cooperate with customs in developing audit, compliance assessment, and account management approaches to achieve the goals of higher compliance, faster processing, and lower costs.

- Review internal systems as well as the systems of your suppliers and other partners in the trade process to ensure that these systems are producing outputs that will be in compliance with customs laws.

- Provide insight to customs on practices in other countries as they pertain to customs audit and account management.

- Perform your own audit and compliance assessment to determine the extent to which your systems, records, and imports to customs are in compliance with customs and other government agency requirements.

Changing a system that has been thought to have worked well over a period of years, even centuries, is a major undertaking. Customs is on the threshold of making significant progress in its approach to its work and dealing with its trading partners. The business community can be a beneficiary of these changes as well as a catalyst for change. Once again, mutual trust and confidence are the keys.

NOTE

1. Stan Davis, *Future Perfect* (Reading, Mass.: Addison-Wesley, 1996), 95.

CHAPTER 10

Risk Management

Concepts of minimum intervention based on information based selectivity and risk analysis, the use of automation, the development of Memoranda of Understanding with our private sector partners, the development of mechanisms for swift resolution of disputes, and the adoption of standardized documentation and definitions are all examples of what we regard as best practice within the global Customs environment.
                                          —James W. Shaver, Secretary General,
                                               World Customs Organization[1]

Government leaders, policy makers, legislators, economists, and business-men frequently overlook the complexity and importance of customs in the global economy. They fail to understand that the principles of free trade and the enforcement of trade agreements can be faithfully and fully executed by a customs administration that has modernized, automated, and implemented all international customs conventions and agreements; sabotaged by a customs administration that is corrupt, inept, or antiquated; and frustrated by a customs that is inconsistent or implements and enforces without the use of advanced measurement and targeting tools.

Customs is not an easy job. In fact, customs requires a knowledge of the classification, value, and origin of virtually all goods produced around the world. When chemicals or medical supplies are being examined, customs is chemistry and biology. When the issue is computers or telecommunications, customs is state-of-the-art high technology and engineering. In this chapter, techniques in compliance measurement and risk management are introduced and their application to the customs environment is examined.

COMPLIANCE MEASUREMENT

While customs is as old as science itself, it has frequently been slow to apply science and advanced business techniques to customs work. Such is the case with the application of statistics to measure compliance against customs goals.

Random sampling, stratified sampling, and other statistical approaches are available to customs to precisely measure the success of customs in achiev-ing its compliance goals. Many customs, probably most customs systems, do not employ statisticians who can establish the parameters for a compliance measurement program. As part of a plan to modernize, customs should em-ploy statistical processes and statisticians to design compliance measurement programs for its cargo and passenger operations.

It is not feasible to measure every aspect of customs compliance but a com-pliance measurement program can be initiated to measure classification com-pliance for all imported goods for every tariff item, valuation compliance and the revenue gap caused by noncompliance, passenger compliance for customs and agriculture requirements, and compliance of carriers, warehouses, and foreign trade zones. For the measurement to be valid, compliance measurement inspections and examinations must be of a precision and rigor not often possessed by customs. Customs inspectors must inspect the exact passenger, entry, conveyance, or shipment designated and perform the inspection or examination in such a way as to ensure its validity. In areas in which the number of entries is small, the complexity is high, and the risk is great, compliance measurement may not be the best alternative.

Measurement is not an end in itself. The purpose of measurement is to determine success and progress toward meeting goals, pinpoint areas of low compliance, and provide information to improve processes and strengthen enforcement. Based on the results of compliance measurement, customs works with the trade community to design programs to increase compliance. Customs action based on compliance measurement results may be any of the following:

- a change in a process
- the establishment of a process improvement team
- cooperation with industry on a compliance program
- the development of an enforcement action
- the establishment of priorities for enforcement and compliance initiatives
- a combination of the above

Compliance measurement is also an input to itself, in that areas of noncompliance are measured more frequently and intensively and high-compliance areas are sampled less frequently.

Compliance measurement is a powerful tool to advance progress toward the goal of a modernized customs administration achieving compliance with all customs laws. It is the first step in introducing a risk management program that can increase certainty that the systems for processing, targeting, inspecting, and auditing are producing the result of higher and higher compliance, faster clearance through customs, and lower costs of compliance.

RISK MANAGEMENT

Peter L. Bernstein, in *Against the Gods: The Remarkable Story of Risk*, says, "The essence of risk management lies in *maximizing the areas where we have some control over the outcome* while minimizing the areas where we have absolutely no control over the outcome and the linkage between effect and cause is hidden from us."[2] Most law enforcement agencies address crime problems and violations that are reported by the public (e.g., murder, robbery, and burglary). In contrast, most customs violations go unreported. Customs crimes, such as narcotics trafficking, money laundering, fraud, and contraband smuggling, are not "victimless crimes," but, because the victim is generally not an individual or group which observes the crime or is directly impacted by it, customs crimes are not routinely brought to the attention of the appropriate authorities. Customs' job then is to uncover the silent, unreported violations out of the massive traffic crossing the nation's borders, the literally millions of transactions that cross each border each year.

In many ways, risk management, customs modernization efforts in general, and ICMP in particular are all about narrowing the gap between those areas where customs has some control over the outcome and some knowledge of cause and effect and those areas where control and knowledge are absent. Customs managers and employees are on a constant search for new technologies and techniques to help them minimize risk in an occupation where risk is inherently high. Compliance measurement can help pinpoint areas of high risk, but it would be foolish to believe that compliance measurement can identify and measure all problems of customs noncompliance. Compliance measurement is particularly weak in areas of deliberate, criminal noncompliance, where violators will take extreme steps to avoid identification and detection, including nonreporting to customs, bribery, smuggling between the ports of entry, free riding on legitimate entries or conveyances, and extreme disguise and subterfuge. In these cases, customs must develop methods for identifying the risk and method of violation and methods for minimizing the risk.

Every element of ICMP is geared toward minimizing the risk that a customs transaction is in some way criminal or not in compliance with customs or other agency laws, as shown in the following examples:

- In the environmental assessment, customs is searching for indications both internally and externally, domestically and internationally of crime problems that may manifest themselves as criminal violations or other noncompliance at the nation's borders.

- An essential outcome of developing customs expertise is the ability of customs officers to identify and detect customs violations in seemingly legitimate commercial shipments. While this has been characterized as the customs "sixth sense," this ability to ferret out the suspicious shipment is more accurately the product of years of training and experience and in more recent years the application of technology and improved techniques. Risk management, data analysis, and automation allows this experience and sixth sense to be shared by the entire organization.

- By increasing integrity and maintaining a workforce and environment free of corruption, customs reduces one of its primary risks and eliminates one of the criminals' and violators' favored means of achieving their objectives.

- Process management contains built-in measures, which include not only measures of cost and cycle time but also measures of compliance, which ensure that risk is minimized in several areas in the organization's major core functions.

- Automation and data analysis provide an opportunity to minimize risk through improved analytical tools made possible by data warehouse and analytical techniques.

These capabilities allow customs to array data from various sources to uncover anomalies, patterns, and inconsistencies that may indicate or uncover violations.

- New techniques in enforcement described in ICMP are geared specifically to managing risk by identifying high-risk areas and categorizing problems by severity of risk and developing countermeasures to prevent violations.

- The objective of audit and account measurement is to go to the center of the system that creates imports for major importers and to ensure that that system is providing customs with information and entries that are in compliance with all customs laws. When customs has this assurance that its major companies are in compliance, it can begin reallocating resources and testing other organizations and entities for level of risk.

- Whether it is called informed compliance, industry partnership, or outreach, it is clear that many customs organizations are working more closely with their industry counterparts to enlist their support in preventing customs violations. These programs range from informal meetings to formal arrangements in which customs provides training and reviews the processes and security of importer and carrier systems to ensure that risk to cargo security, terrorist devices, or smuggling attempts are minimized.

In addition to the elements of ICMP designed to incorporate measures to minimize risk, customs administrations around the world are appealing to the general public to provide information to reduce smuggling. These programs include toll-free numbers, general meetings with community organizations, and rewards for information on smuggling incidents and organizations. Customs is also employing technology and innovation to minimize risk, including large scale and mobile x-ray sensor systems, video surveillance, narcotics and money detector canines, and profile systems. These systems are geared toward separating the high from the low risk and to providing a deterrent to smuggling and other violations.

CONCLUSION

Customs now has an unprecedented opportunity to increase its effectiveness, improve compliance, and minimize risk even in the face of an enormously large workloads. By the judicious and intelligent application of compliance measurement and the risk management techniques outlined in this chapter and throughout ICMP, customs can systematically measure compliance levels in key areas and develop plans to increase compliance while shifting focus and resources to areas of low and unknown compliance. Success in customs compliance and enforcement are greatly enhanced by new technology and the application of data analysis techniques, but violators are also sophisticated and employ much of the same and sometimes better technology in a more agile and innovative fashion. By defining the universe of violator and smuggling opportunities, customs can categorize and prioritize risk by severity and frequency and develop a comprehensive strategy for dealing with risk.

Recommendations from Chapter 10

- Develop a competency in compliance measurement.
- Establish a baseline of compliance by measuring the entire tariff schedule.
- Develop compliance improvement plans and problem-solving initiatives for commodities and industries with low compliance.
- Focus future compliance measurement and compliance improvement initiatives on areas of low compliance and high priority.
- Reduce inspection levels in high-compliance areas.
- Develop competence in risk management.
- Focus problem-solving and enforcement efforts on areas of high risk.
- Develop plans to minimize risk with first priorities in areas of greatest vulnerability.

Actions for Global Customs Managers for Chapter 10

In many ways, the entire approach of the International Customs Modernization Process is to manage and minimize risk. Each element of ICMP contributes in some way to segregating the high risk from the low risk. This represents a transformation in the way customs transacts business and it is an approach with which not all customs are yet comfortable. Business has applied risk management and measurement approaches for many years. The banking, finance, and insurance industries are based on risk management. Global trade partners can help customs, and thus themselves, in this transition in several ways:

- Share the experience of your business and industry with customs.
- Participate with customs in the elements of ICMP to lay the foundation for a formal risk management and compliance measurement approach.
- Welcome customs review of your systems, records, and practices worldwide.
- Provide customs the benefit of your insights on customs risk management practices around the world.
- Assess your own systems and compliance levels and take necessary steps to improve those systems and your compliance record.
- Encourage other government agencies to adopt risk management, compliance assessment, and measurement approaches to their work at the borders and in the import and export process.

The outcome of these actions is to build mutual trust and confidence based on shared data and proven mathematical and statistical sciences. The end result is higher compliance for customs and reduced cost and faster service for industry. This is consistent with sage advice from the Middle East: "Trust in Allah, but tie your camel."

NOTES

1. James W. Shaver, Speech to Customs Reform and Modernization Forum, World Customs Organization, Brussels, April 28, 1997.

2. Peter L. Bernstein, *Against the Gods: The Remarkable Story of Risk* (New York: John Wiley & Sons, 1996), 197.

CHAPTER 11

Implement

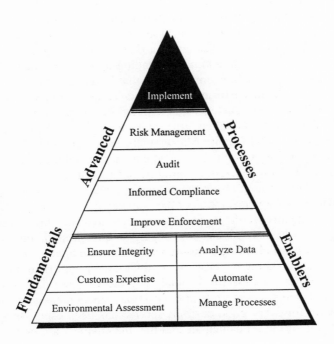

The job of the leader is to fix destinations, to solve problems, to preserve values, to create climates in which people can and want to give their best.

—Donald E. Walker,
Never Try to Teach a Pig to Sing[1]

The first obligation of leadership is to create an environment which enables employees to make their best contribution to the mission and goals of the organization. The International Customs Modernization Process was designed to help the leadership of customs create such an environment within their organizations. Customs leaders create that environment by doing the following:

- ensuring that the workplace is free of corruption
- establishing a clear direction, vision, and goals for the organization and its employees
- encouraging and rewarding teamwork to achieve the goals of the organization
- obtaining the budget, resources, and technology necessary to accomplish the mission and goals
- providing employees with the skills and training needed to excel in their profession

Many excellent plans for management and organizational improvement fail in implementation. Good ideas and good intentions must be translated into an implementation plan and meticulously monitored if success is to be achieved. Every customs organization in the world should be in a constant state of modernization and improvement. The starting point and methodology will vary from one customs service to another depending upon their state of development. For example, a customs organization that is very sound on fundamentals—that is, has been performing an effective environmental scan, has developed and maintained customs expertise, has developed strong safeguards for individual and institutional integrity, and has implemented Business Process Management, Total Quality Management, automation, and data analysis—should be prepared for the advanced customs techniques.

For those customs organizations initiating a fundamental customs reform and modernization program from the ground up, the recommended approach is to start with dual implementation of the fundamentals and enablers. On one track, customs teams would be performing the environmental assessment, developing plans to increase customs expertise, and strengthening customs integrity. On a parallel track, customs would be introducing the BPM and TQM processes, updating or initiating automation and information technology, and developing a capacity for analyzing the valuable data in customs files and automated systems. Only after customs management is satisfied that the foundation for every good customs service has been established by the implementation of the fundamentals and that the enablers are on the path to successful implementation should the advanced techniques be implemented. Customs must also be supported in the modernization effort by national leadership in the treasury or finance department and elsewhere in the national government. This is the political will necessary for customs reform.

For all customs administrations, regardless of their state of development, customs modernization is a continuous process. The environmental assessment and the updating of customs skills and expertise never cease. The very idea of BPM and TQM is to introduce the concept of continuous improvement and long-term commitment. Automated systems must be updated as improvements are made in information technology. Successful implementation will require a long-term commitment to improvement and mechanisms to guide the organization through the change and modernization process. A strategic plan can be an important mechanism for ICMP implementation. A strategic plan typically provides for a five-year planning horizon. Annual one-year plans are derived from the strategic plan. The organization responsible for overseeing the implementation of the modernization plan should be the Executive Improvement Team, chaired by the Director General or Chief Operating Officer, as described previously. The idea of a "team" leading the change and modernization effort is a good one, as it sets an example that crossfunctional and interdisciplinary teams are the key to success in all modern, complex organizations in business or government.

The strategic plan need not be and should not be an elaborate document. It should clearly set out the direction of the organization, reemphasizing the mission, purpose, values, and goals. The annual plan will provide the one-year objectives for implementation toward the long-range goals. The following is a guideline for implementation:

- Institute an EIT composed of high-level operational executives to oversee the change and modernization process. The EIT should be chaired by the Director General of Customs or the Chief Operating Officer.
- Establish and publish a strategic plan which sets out the direction and goals of the modernization process.
- Review the mission statement, values, long-range goals, and code of conduct in light of the change effort. Modify these elements as appropriate based on the goals of the modernization effort and the strategic plan. Communicate with employees at all levels and by all means, but particularly in face-to-face meetings.
- Involve employees and managers in the process but remember that setting the direction of the organization, its values, and goals is a particular function of top management.
- Keep the process open and have frequent meetings with managers and employees on the status and progress of the process.
- Include private sector counterparts in the process (e.g., importers, exporters, brokers, port authorities, warehousemen, zone operators, etc.) and incorporate their input.
- Implement one-year and short-term goals through crossfunctional teams and hold teams accountable for meeting milestones.

- Stick with the plan and objectives but be open to new opportunities as they are identified.

- Establish goals that are moderately challenging; research indicates that motivation to achieve is greatest when goals challenge but are perceived as achievable and fair.

- Ensure that modernization is consistent with WCO programs to include the Columbus Declaration, the Nairobi Convention, the Koyoto Convention, and the International Chamber of Commerce Customs Guidelines.

- Take advantage of the tremendous improvement in information technology to leverage modernization efforts and to improve organizational effectiveness and compliance.

- Get input from outside sources, such as the WCO, other customs, and the business community, but maintain control over the process.

- Define your core competencies (i.e., those skills that are essential to the long-range success of the organization, such as customs expertise), and give particular attention to developing skills in those areas. Consider contracting out for other skills and competencies from others who are best in the world in that skill and gradually capture knowledge from contractors and consultants.

- Concentrate on developing world-class customs expertise first and then develop competencies in automation, information technology, data analysis, audit, measurement, and risk management. Bring in experts in those fields and ensure transfer of knowledge to the organization. Consider hiring new classes of employees with skills in analysis, measurement, audit, and risk management.

Implementation of ICMP along these lines will increase compliance with customs and other agency laws at the border, reduce the cost of compliance to government and industry, and reduce cycle times for legitimate goods and travelers. ICMP will be a source of pride for employees as their work is given greater meaning by making measurable contributions to important national goals. ICMP will contribute to the wealth and prosperity of your nation by making it a more desirable location for trade and investment, and it will establish customs as the foundation in the worldwide fight against transnational crime.

Top management's role in ICMP is to provide leadership by setting the direction, establishing the goals, defining the boundaries, measuring the progress, and ensuring the balance between creativity and control. At the 1997 Customs/Trade/Finance Symposium of the Americas, James W. Shaver, Secretary General of the World Customs Organization made the following comments on customs reform and modernization. His words provide inspiration for those customs administrations initiating a reform and modernization program.

I know that many of you may be thinking to yourselves—Well is this all just theory or does it really work? It is our experience that when customs administrations undertake such fundamental change the outcomes are extremely positive. Processing times and inspection rates are reduced, interaction with the business community is improved, there is an improved public image, revenue yields increase and the use of automation provides for opportunities such as the introduction of prearrival release consignments.

I can do little better than draw your attention to the achievement of Peruvian Customs who instituted a reform package that has now resulted in a reduction in clearance time from 5 days to 2 hours and a reduction of inspection from up to 100% to 15%. That is a remarkable transformation and a similar success story has emerged in Uganda where with WCO assistance they have reduced their time spent processing consignments by more than 60% against a background of a 20% lift in revenue.

These are efficiency gains that are achievable but it requires a great deal of planning, determination and cooperation between the government and private sector, and that means a lot of hard work and tenacity by all involved. But I believe it is worth it if you want to develop that competitive edge in international trade.[2]

Actions for Global Customs Managers for Chapter 11

Management change specialists are fond of comparisons and metaphors of the change process, such as saying an effort is comparable to "changing a tire speeding down a freeway at sixty miles an hour" or "overhauling a 747 aircraft in flight." However, any system responsible for the movement and regulation of over $5 trillion worth of goods and hundreds of millions of passengers each year requires no marketing or hyperbole to prove its importance. The importance of global trade is exemplified by actions of governments and world leaders to position their countries to share in the benefits of the new global trade system.

Customs reform and modernization plays a big role in improving that system. For too long, some customs administrations have served as barriers to legitimate trade comparable to feudal systems of the past, thus fragmenting what should be an integrated worldwide system. The seams in what would be a seamless system have sometimes been inept, corrupt, antiquated, and protectionist customs organizations. In other cases, the seams have been customs practices not in conformance with international standards. On the industry side, there has been frustration, a willingness to tolerate substandard practices, corruption equal to that of customs, a shortsightedness on the need for worldwide integration, and a failure to engage with customs to achieve worldwide customs reform and modernization.

For the first time, government and industry are seeing both the need and the benefits for customs to represent national sovereignty at the borders, provide needed revenues for developing economies, and facilitate the standardized integrated worldwide trade process. The WCO has provided the leadership to establish the global standards and to bring together the WTO, UNCTAD, World Bank officials, and the business community in an effort to reform and modernize. The political will is being provided by heads of state. The momentum is leading to reform, but will require the pressure and persistence of the business community in the following forms:

- engagement of the business community with customs and other government agencies at the international, regional, and local levels

- support of the WCO and its leadership in customs reform (some governments, the United States foremost among them, have failed to pay their dues to the WCO)
- establishing partnerships with customs in the modernization initiative
- encouraging and prodding national leaders to support customs reform in their countries and to provide the political will for continued customs modernization
- supporting customs and customs systems as the focal point for modernization of the global trade system
- providing guidance to customs in application of new technology and improved processing techniques while maintaining uniformity and consistency with international conventions and standards

This is a big task, but the reward is more than the billions in annual savings. It is increased health, prosperity, and security for all nations. The International Customs Modernization Process is an integrating mechanism and catalyst for making this potential a reality.

NOTES

1. Donald E. Walker, *Never Try to Teach a Pig to Sing* (San Diego: Lathrop Press, 1996), 30.

2. James W. Shaver, Speech to Customs Reform and Modernization Forum, World Customs Organization, Brussels, April 28, 1997.

CHAPTER 12

The Future

Because of what we have learned from the notion of economic interdependence, I believe we are on the threshold of a global revolution. The benefits of a global marketplace, combined with effective international institutions, will set humanity on a course of increasing prosperity through technological innovation and societal evolution that we can scarcely dream of. The competition of goods and services, combined with the competition of ideas, scientific research and development, hold out the prospect of changes within years that centuries have not accomplished.
—Donald Johnson, Secretary General of the OECD[1]

Customs administrations are organizations that can trace their history not in decades or centuries, but in millennia. Such longevity provides a degree of perspective in an era that is characterized by fast-paced change and scientific and technological advances perhaps unprecedented in the history of mankind. While fierce competition—local, national, and international—is creating paranoia among companies, countries, and labor, customs is comparatively insulated by the protection of governments and centuries of tradition. But customs has not been totally immune from change, and the comparatively recent and exponential increases in world travel and trade coupled with the advances in technology and transportation are combining to focus the attention of world leaders and multinational companies on the purpose, functions, actions, effectiveness, and efficiency of customs at the borders. For the benefit of their nations and their employees, customs must respond with modernization initiatives that are equal to the demands of an increasingly integrated global economy.

Customs faces a number of demanding challenges from globalization. Extreme increases in the volume of border transactions (entries, passengers, and conveyances), which have been customs traditional view of its workload, are the most obvious and most often discussed. Demands for facilitation and faster and faster cycle times and release times accompany the crushing workloads. Just-in-time delivery systems, air express cargo shipments, multibillion-dollar intermodal transportation systems, and port cargo handling complexes represent trillion-dollar investments in fast cargo delivery that fuels the international trading systems. Government and industry leaders are becoming less tolerant of antiquated customs systems that stand in the way of global best practices and integrated multinational industries. Along with the volumes of trade and the extensive participation of new players and industries comes a complexity that requires customs to look at merchandise and processes from all corners of the globe and every product under the sun.

New regional trade agreements further complicate the picture. Trade agreements introduced to facilitate and lower trade barriers add another level of complexity for customs officers who now must familiarize themselves with preference programs and ensure that applicants and goods meet increasingly complex origin rules. In the Americas alone, the Organization of America States counts nineteen regional trade agreements. Adding more complexity to the customs picture are the increasing demands, some by business and some by governments, for more protection at the borders for the environment, health, safety, antiterrorism, and intellectual property. An additional dimension of complexity and concern is introduced by the specter of transnational crime and transnational criminal organizations trafficking in narcotics, contraband, weapons, and the illicit proceeds of criminal activity threatening the viability of some countries and the integrity of the international banking system. Attacking these compound and interrelated problems is a colossal task.

These are just some of the daunting tasks and challenges faced by customs around the world. Are customs administrations around the world equal to these challenges, particularly when they are expected to manage their operations with static or even declining resources and budgets? This question can be answered with surprising optimism for a variety of reasons. First and foremost, the future of the ideal world customs has been outlined with stunning clarity by the WCO. Perhaps in no other profession in government or in industry has the ideal state been better or more clearly defined as it has been for customs. Each and every customs administration has merely to properly implement the following to enter the top echelon of customs around the world:

- The Harmonized System of Classification
- The WTO's Value Code
- The Nairobi Convention
- The Arusha Declaration
- The Columbus Declaration
- The ICC Customs Guidelines
- UNEDIFACT-Based Automated Systems
- The Kyoto Convention on the Simplification and Harmonization of Customs Procedures (under revision)

Implementation of these international standards and conventions is the foundation for the successful customs administration (defined as an organization that is approaching 100-percent compliance with customs and government laws at the border), and is reducing the cost of compliance and cycle times for government and industry. As these standards and conventions are uniformly implemented around the world, each nation benefits and tens of billions of dollars will be saved annually as uniform worldwide systems replace antiquated, unique, manual national systems.

Customs administrations now have the tools in the WCO's Customs Reform and Modernization Program and the International Customs Modernization Process to assist in the uniform implementation of a modernization program. Modern technological tools in automation and advanced business practices can now be applied to customs systems to leverage customs to new levels of effectiveness. ICMP outlines each of those tools and practices. A two- to five-year commitment is needed to implement these programs.

While implementation of all these tools is essential, it does not signal the end of the modernization initiative. Implementation of all of the international customs conventions and systems is the beginning of a modernization process. The pace of change will continue to accelerate as advances in technology increase. Global trade will continue to expand as China, Russia, and the countries of the former Soviet Union are joined by the emerging economies in South America and Africa yearning to improve the quality of life for their citizens by participation in global trade. Business will continue to seek comparative advantage and locate in countries where infrastructure, labor, government policies, and customs provide the most enlightened business environment. The volume of travel and trade will continue to increase. At the same time, criminal organizations will become richer, smarter, more powerful, better networked, and employ better technology and increase their influence on some industries and governments. The future becomes harder to predict as time horizons are longer, but it is clear that those governments and customs that fail to modernize now are sentencing their nations to life on the fringe and margins of the future world economy.

In addition to the steps outlined herein, the prudent customs service will be taking the following actions to ensure the prosperity of its nation:

- investing heavily and wisely in information technology to process the increased transactions of the future
- developing a database which will be the source of information for the nation and customs on all aspects of their nation's international trade
- developing a capability in advanced analytical techniques that will result in increased compliance of legitimate importers and better targeting against violators and violations
- developing competencies in compliance measurement and risk management to ensure that valuable resources are brought to bear on priority problems and vulnerabilities
- reinvesting their personnel to work in high-risk areas, allowing automated systems to handle routine processing and developing skills in data analysis, audit, automation, and advanced enforcement techniques
- developing partnerships with other government agencies and other customs administrations to form an alliance against international crime and international criminal organizations
- enlisting the support of industry in the fight against international trafficking in narcotics, weapons, contraband, money laundering, terrorism, and customs fraud, including intellectual property rights violations
- developing information partnerships with other customs administrations so that export data of one customs is the foundation for import data for the other
- participating in the exchange of information, databases, and e-mail among the world's customs administrations on criminal violations and criminal organizations
- automating and providing real-time access to other governments and industry information on all customs tariffs, rulings, procedures, and processes
- developing a capacity for performing best practices and other modern business techniques that will ensure that customs remains at the leading edge of modern customs practices
- contributing dollars, support, and participation in the World Customs Organization as the focal point for worldwide customs improvement, coordination, standardization, and modernization

Achieving this will ensure that your customs administration is prepared for whatever the future may hold, and will ensure that your customs administration contributes to the wealth of your nation.

World leaders sign international trade agreements. Heads of state ratify international conventions on commerce. But to paraphrase an American politician, all customs is local. It is the individual customs administration in partnership with their national trade community which either implements the various trade agreements and conventions or ignores them. International conventions on customs classification, value, and procedure (and soon origin) have been supplemented by fundamentally redundant declarations signed in cities such as Columbus, Washington (see Appendix H), and Ottawa (see Appendix I). The time has come for implementation.

ICMP provides the mechanism for national customs and industry to make these conventions real. Economic prosperity provides the incentive to modernize. The WCO and the WTO provide the leadership. National leaders, customs directors general, and global trade managers must provide the political will for implementation in order to bring the benefits of free trade to each nation and to companies everywhere. A new alliance, led by the WTO, the WCO, and the ICC, should be established to monitor and to report on annual progress in compliance with international customs agreements to ensure implementation.

NOTES

If you are interested in obtaining more information on customs modernization or would like to provide information, examples, or case studies, or, if you would like to obtain a copy of the *Handbook on Customs Modernization*, an abridged version of the book in booklet form, please contact the author:

> 6723 N. 25th Street
> Arlington, Va. 22213
> Telephone: (703) 534–1369
> Fax: (703) 534–7160

1. Donald Johnson, cited in James W. Shaver's speech, Customs Reform and Modernization Forum, World Customs Organization, Brussels, April 28, 1997.

PART IV

APPENDIXES

ICC Guidelines

 International Chamber of Commerce
The world business organization

International Customs Guidelines

Prepared by the Committee on Customs and Trade Regulation

INTRODUCTION

These Guidelines, an initial business contribution to the implementation of the ICC Cooperation Agreement (1996) with the World Customs Organisation (WCO), present a comprehensive set of practices which the ICC considers are of particular value and importance for those engaged in international trade and transport and should characterise all modern customs administrations.

The Guidelines draw on a range of documents established by the WCO, including the Kyoto Convention and the Columbus Declaration. Many of their recommended practices—for example, the use of risk-assessment techniques with pre-entry and post-audit procedures—are as favourable to more effective customs control as to improved trade facilitation. The Guidelines make specific reference to the value of systematic customs/trade cooperation through Memorandum of Understanding programmes.

The Guidelines will have many uses. They set out, in a convenient and well-defined form, a summary list of key procedures which can be readily expanded into a comprehensive Code of Best Customs Practices, which would be of considerable value to customs and trade in many emerging and transition economies. They should prove most useful as a means of rapid analysis of customs quality by such lending agencies as the World Bank or the IMF, for which international trade performance, greatly influenced by customs efficiency, is a key factor in financing and loan assessments.

They can serve as the basis for a regular review and classification of customs services and as a reliable index of their progress. They look ahead to certain potential extensions of current practice, and so provide signposts to customs innovations.

They will, of course, be adapted over a period to reflect new trading, transport and administrative techniques, particularly in respect of information and communication technologies. The ICC expects to gain much from experience of their use, in their present form, in European transitional economies and in the focal customs activities now under way in APEC and NAFTA.

They are a powerful tool to help bring practical freedom for the individual international transaction into line with the policy objective of global trade liberalisation.

Certain procedures may not be feasible at the moment, in some countries, by reason of legal constraints. It is no part of the ICC intention to ask customs to question national legislation, but all the points set out in the Guidelines have satisfactory practical application by some leading customs administrations and the ICC advances such proposals in the expectation that any remaining legal obstacles, elsewhere, will be progressively removed.

The Guidelines in no way imply any reduction in the responsibilities of traders to comply fully with customs laws and regulations. Indeed, they are intended to encourage cooperation between customs and commerce so that both can fulfil their obligations without conflict.

THE GUIDELINES

A modern, efficient and effective customs administration:

CHECKLIST

Ticks in the box against every Guideline with which a customs service complies can provide a summary guide to efficiency. Crosses can identify non-compliance. Space is provided for comments on reasons for deficiencies, possibilities of improvement, etc.

A. Strategic Plan

1. associates its business community with the development of a strategic plan, looking forward three to five years, which describes its overall strategy and key priorities, supported by an annual management plan containing more detailed targets, objectives and performance measures;

2. publishes an annual review, up-dating strategy and reporting progress;

B. Workforce and Structure

3. employs a highly professional workforce, which is recruited competitively, well trained, adequately paid and screened for enforcement risks, with written, standardised job descriptions and objectives, supporting transparent career development and promotion policies;

4. establishes an internal security unit, or is subject to an equivalent external body, to deal with issues of employee integrity. These arrangements should be known to the trade community, which should be given information enabling them to contact the appropriate security agency as and when necessary;

5. ensures that all employees having contact with the public carry proper identification, which should be shown on request;

6. employs, trains and identifies, as appropriate, tariff classification, valuation and rules of origin experts, to assist the trade community in these areas;

7. trains officers to investigate complex frauds, and recommMend appropriate action;

C. Cargo Processing (General)

8. applies the WCO Kyoto Convention and actively supports current WCO work on its review and revision;

A. Strategic Plan

[1] _____
_____
_____
_____
_____
_____
_____
_____
_____

[2] _____
_____

B. Workforce and Structure

[3] _____
_____
_____
_____
_____
_____
_____
_____

[4] _____
_____
_____
_____
_____
_____
_____
_____

[5] _____
_____
_____
_____

[6] _____
_____
_____
_____

[7] _____
_____
_____

C. Cargo Processing (General)

[8] _____
_____
_____

D. Cargo Processing (Inwards)

D. Cargo Processing (Inwards)

9. relates physical control procedures to documentary control procedures, in such a way that essential control data are processed in advance of the arrival of the goods, while other, administrative data are handled by post-clearance controls;

[9] _____

10. gives the declarant the option to secure immediate or rapid release by filing entry data in advance of the arrival of the goods;

[10] _____

11. gives the declarant the option to enter data, either manually or electronically, and comply with essential control requirements, at a place different from the location of the goods;

[11] _____

12. establishes control and release systems that enable the importer or agent to obtain the goods prior to the completion of administrative requirements and payment of duties, taxes and fees;

[12] _____

13. applies the WCO Express Guidelines for consignments for which immediate or expedited release or clearance is requested, regardless of weight, value, size, type of operator or carrier, or mode of transport;

[13] _____

14. applies a *de-minimis* regime whereby certain goods, including documents, private gift packages and trade samples, not exceeding a certain value or weight, are exempted from import duties and taxes and from formal declaration procedures;

[14] _____

15. reviews *de-minimis* levels regularly to take account of such factors as inflation;

[15] _____

16. gives the importer the option to file entries himself or to use an authorized agent;

[16] _____

17. releases goods at carrier's point of arrival, without requiring their interim transfer to a government-operated or -designated warehouse;

[17] _____

18. uses selectivity, based on automated compliance measurement and risk-assessment and profiling systems, to target suspect consignments and so minimise the incidence of physical examinations;

    [18] _____
_____
_____
_____
_____
_____

19. operates a corporate surety bonding system, or other appropriate means, such as a duty- and tax-deferral system, to protect the revenue and ensure compliance with customs laws without unnecessarily delaying the release of goods;

    [19] _____
_____
_____
_____
_____
_____
_____

20. fixes, in the absence of any evidence of fraud, a reasonable limit on the time during which it can demand additional duties and/or the re-delivery of the goods;

    [20] _____
_____
_____
_____
_____

21. develops the use of non-intrusive examination techniques, such as X-ray;

    [21] _____
_____

22. develops and applies performance standards to check that its processing and release of goods are timely and meet reasonable business needs;

    [22] _____
_____
_____
_____

23. allows authorized importers to file single entries covering all their importations in a given period, e.g., monthly;

    [23] _____
_____
_____

24. replaces transaction-by-transaction treatment by account-based, post-entry procedures for importers with proven compliance histories and consistent import patterns (e.g., types of goods and origins);

    [24] _____
_____
_____
_____
_____
_____

25. has government authority to perform certain control functions, at the time of import, for other official agencies and links these agencies to customs automated systems and databases for targeting and risk-assessment purposes;

    [25] _____
_____
_____
_____
_____
_____

26. adapts its working hours to ascertained commercial needs and operational requirements, and operates any necessary overtime or other exceptional service systems on transparent cost bases negotiated with business clients;

    [26] _____
_____
_____
_____
_____
_____

E. Cargo Processing (Outwards)

27. ensures that the statistical requirements for recording purposes are not
applied in ways, or at times or places,
that could significantly affect the efficiency of the export operation;

28. accepts, as far as possible, a commercial document, e.g., invoice, containing the necessary particulars, as the
export declaration, in place of an official form;

F. Cargo Processing (Transit)

29. applies appropriate international transit conventions, for example, those
noted in Annex E.1 of the Kyoto Convention;

30. cooperates closely with other neighbouring customs administrations to
assist effective control and facilitation of common transit traffic;

31. operates computerised systems providing early, reliable notice of dis-
charge of declarants', carriers' and
guarantors' transit obligations and
effective means of identifying and
preventing fraud;

32. accepts that guarantees or deposits for
the transit operation remove any need
for supplementary undertakings or
payments at point of entry;

G. Transparency of Regulation and Administration

33. publishes its strategic plan and all customs regulations and makes them available to the public through the most
modern and practical media, while ensuring that existing and new regulations
and legislation are simple in form, content and presentation;

34. consults the trade community, systematically, to obtain views on proposed

E. Cargo Processing (Outwards)

[27] _____
_____
_____
_____
_____

[28] _____
_____
_____
_____
_____

F. Cargo Processing (Transit)

[29] _____
_____
_____
_____

[30] _____
_____
_____
_____

[31] _____
_____
_____
_____
_____
_____

[32] _____
_____
_____
_____

G. Transparency of Regulation and Administration

[33] _____
_____
_____
_____
_____
_____
_____

[34] _____
_____

new regulations and procedures, or amendments to existing requirements, and gives them timely notice of any eventual changes;

35. adopts a Memoranda of Understanding programme, based upon that sponsored by the WCO, by which improved co-operation with the trade community is established in the areas of information exchange, security and training, with a view to more effective interdiction of customs fraud, in particular drug trafficking, infringements of intellectual property rights and threats to endangered species;

[35] _____

36. provides the means for the trade community to question or appeal decisions, by local officials, to a higher level, within customs, and, eventually, to a court of law, settling minor violations, normally, at the local level;

[36] _____

37. establishes an ombudsman, specialised in customs matters, as a medium for approaching the administration and a general information office or section to deal with queries from the trading community;

[37] _____

H. Automation

H. Automation

38. operates a nationwide automated system to provide electronic filing facilities for the trade community in respect of declaration data to be submitted at both import and export and for banks and corporate sureties in respect of duty and tax guarantees and surety bonds

[38] _____

39. is able to transmit and receive data, nationally and internationally, using appropriate international EDI standards;

[39] _____

40. provides automated systems for the payment of duties, taxes and other fees by electronic fund transfer;

[40] _____

41. makes tariff and related information/ data available to the trading community from an automated system;

[41] _____

42. establishes and operates an automated enforcement information system, using risk assessment and other modern control techniques;

[42] _____
_____
_____
_____

43. requires, as a matter of routine, in automated systems, only those data items which can be clearly linked to significant gains in customs operational efficiency;

[43] _____
_____
_____
_____
_____

I. Tariff Classification and Valuation

I. Tariff Classification and Valuation

44. applies the WCO Harmonised System Convention;

[44] _____
_____

45. applies the WTO Valuation Agreement;

[45] _____

46. issues binding pre-entry classification and valuation rulings, on request, which will be honoured by officers, throughout the customs territory;

[46] _____
_____
_____
_____

47. identifies and makes available customs experts to advise the trade community on tariff classification and valuation matters;

[47] _____
_____
_____
_____

48. provides a sound, scientific basis for classification decisions through the use of laboratory analysis, equipment and technology;

[48] _____
_____
_____
_____

49. publishes tariff classification and valuation rulings, either in printed form or on electronic media, and makes them available to traders and other customs administrations;

[49] _____
_____
_____
_____
_____

J. Origin

J. Origin

50. publishes current origin rules and rulings;

[50] _____
_____

51. applies, in due course, the WTO Rules of Origin;

[51] _____
_____

K. Disputes and Sanctions

K. Disputes and Sanctions

52. accepts and applies the penalty regimes in Annex H.2 of the Kyoto Convention;

[52] _____
_____
_____

53. favours the resolution of disputes with traders through conciliation and financial adjustment rather than recourse to courts;

[53] _____

L. International

54. is a WCO member and participates in WCO and regional customs activities;

55. shares information with, and provides technical assistance to, other customs administrations for enforcement and facilitation purposes;

56. consults with major traders/carriers to develop customs/customs/business electronic information systems that would, initially, link and, eventually, replace traditionally separate export and import formalities;

L. International

[54] _____

[55] _____

[56] _____

M. Passenger Processing

57. relies on passenger observation techniques and behaviour profiles rather than routine questioning of all passengers;

58. establishes benchmark standards for passenger processing times and checks performances with corresponding benchmarks in other customs administrations;

59. uses automation techniques, including EDI, to improve the efficiency and security of passenger processing, including, where appropriate, the capture of Advance Passenger Information (API) from machine-readable travel documents, leading to expedited passenger clearance;

60. uses a passenger processing system that is integrated with immigration and other control authorities, in order to avoid procedural duplication.

M. Passenger Processing

[57] _____

[58] _____

[59] _____

[60] _____

Document n° 103/190 Rev.

10 July 1997

Columbus Declaration

**United Nations Conference
on Trade and Development**

Distr.GENERAL
TD/SYMP.TE/6
4 November 1994
Original: ENGLISH

REPORT OF THE UNITED NATIONS INTERNATIONAL SYMPOSIUM ON TRADE EFFICIENCY
held at Columbus, Ohio, from 17 to 21 October 1994

CONTENTS

INTRODUCTION

1. At its eighth session, held in Cartagena de Indias, Colombia, from 8 to 25 February 1992, the United Nations Conference on Trade and Development decided to establish an Ad Hoc Working Group on Trade Efficiency. The Group was to be responsible for producing guidelines needed to take concrete steps towards trade efficiency at the national and international levels, especially in developing countries. The Group was also to identify and formulate the elements necessary to the promotion and implementation of such guidelines, focusing on their legal, technical, procedural and institutional components while preserving full scope for private sector initiatives in this field. The culmination of these efforts of the Group was to be an international symposium on trade efficiency, to be held in 1994. This event was to reinforce international discussion on the promotion of harmonized national and regional infrastructures for trade and trade efficiency. It was to focus especially on the requirements for involving all countries in efficient trade, giving priority to ways and means of promoting the participation of small and medium-sized enterprises in international trade (Cartagena Commitment (TD/346/Rev.1), paras. 157–158).

2. At the second part of its thirty-eighth session, held from 21 April to 7 May 1992, the Trade and Development Board, by its decision 398 (XXXVIII), established the terms of reference for the Ad Hoc Working Group on Trade Efficiency. These terms of reference included the preparation of the 1994 international symposium on trade efficiency, as called for in the Cartagena Commitment. The Ad Hoc Working Group held three sessions, the first from 16 to 20 November 1992, the second from 15 to 19 November 1993, and the third from 2 to 11 May 1994.

3. In its resolution 47/183, of 22 December 1992, the General Assembly endorsed the convening in 1994 of a United Nations international symposium on trade efficiency and requested the Secretary-General of UNCTAD to make all the necessary arrangements for that symposium, taking into account the preparatory work of the Ad Hoc Working Group on Trade Efficiency.

4. At the second part of its thirty-ninth session, held from 15 to 26 March 1993, the Trade and Development Board welcomed and endorsed the holding of the Symposium in Columbus (Ohio), United States of America, in 1994.

5. In accordance with a decision taken by the Ad Hoc Working Group on Trade Efficiency at its third session, a Preparatory Committee for the United Nations International Symposium on Trade Efficiency met from 27 June to 1 July 1994. The Preparatory Committee approved the "Draft Columbus ministerial declaration on trade efficiency" and the "Draft recommendations and guidelines for trade efficiency" for transmission to the International Symposium.

6. The United Nations International Symposium on Trade Efficiency was thus held at Columbus, Ohio, from 17 to 21 October 1994. The Symposium consisted of a Senior Officials Segment, held on 17 and 18 October, and a Ministerial Segment, held from 19 to 21 October. The present report contains the outcome of the Symposium, as well as a brief account of procedural and organizational matters.

Chapter I

COLUMBUS MINISTERIAL DECLARATION
ON TRADE EFFICIENCY*

Preamble

We, the Ministers and representatives of the States members of the United Nations Conference on Trade and Development, assembled in the City of Columbus (Ohio, United States of America) from 17 to 21 October 1994 at the United Nations International Symposium on Trade Efficiency, declare the following:

1. Greater participation in international trade is a prerequisite for development. Dynamic and healthy international trade is a major instrument for the economic growth and sustainable development of all countries. It also contributes to the goals of poverty alleviation and employment creation on a worldwide basis.

2. The historic signing of the Final Act of the Uruguay Round in April 1994 in Marrakesh (Morocco) marked the successful conclusion of many years of negotiations on the macro-economic framework required for the emergence of an open, predictable, secure and non-discriminatory trading system. However, efforts made to secure an open trade environment will not bear their full benefits unless the enterprises of all nations can import and export efficiently. Here in Columbus we have gathered to find solutions to these micro-economic issues of international trade.

3. Over the last few years, significant progress has been made towards the establishment of more open and dynamic trade relations. Many countries, and in particular developing countries and countries in transition, have made significant efforts to liberalize and adjust their trade policies to multilateral disciplines. In this new context, trade efficiency, which allows faster, simpler, broader and less costly trade, is a valuable policy tool: it offers the natural bridge between the broad objectives of enhancing trade and development on one hand and the practical measures necessary to allow the international community to reach such objectives on the other hand.

Efficient trade and development

4. Ensuring that no potential trader is excluded from international trade is a priority objective for the international community as a whole. In all countries, potential traders, especially small and medium-sized enterprises, are confined to the mar-

---

*At its opening plenary meeting, on 19 October 1994, the Symposium adopted the Columbus Ministerial Declaration on Trade Efficiency. At its closing plenary meeting, on 21 October 1994, the Symposium decided to transmit the Columbus Ministerial Declaration on Trade Efficiency and the supporting recommendations and guidelines for trade efficiency to the General Assembly.

gins of international trade because of lack of efficient procedures, lack of access to information and information networks, or inadequate support services or trade logistics. Although the needs to be addressed vary from one country to the next, enterprises of all countries can greatly benefit from higher awareness of efficient business practices and trade facilitation measures. Since such improvements need not be technology-intensive, they can generate substantial benefits at all levels of the development process.

5. Small and medium-sized enterprises, a major instrument of employment creation and technology transfer, need to be better equipped, serviced and trained to export and import more efficiently. Close cooperation among national and local government authorities and enterprise sectors strengthens the ability of these firms to participate fully in international trade.

6. As electronic commerce is rapidly spreading to many sectors of activity and regions of the world, concerted action is required in order to allow all potential traders to rely on simplified, compatible procedures and practices, and to make the best possible use of modern technologies in order to lower the cost of international trade transactions worldwide.

7. Electronic commerce is still an advanced, technology-intensive way to trade; as such, it bears as many opportunities as challenges for the less advanced among the nations of the world. The promotion of electronic commerce worldwide should be based on the principle of equality of access of all countries to systems compatible with the international standards recommended by the United Nations. In order to enhance the participation of developing countries in this new form of trade, special terms of access to electronic networks and business information may be considered. The efforts towards greater efficiency should also contribute to achieving greater equity among trading partners.

8. Adoption of trade efficiency measures can significantly lower the costs of trade transactions. Estimates place the costs of trade transactions at 7 to 10 per cent of the total value of world trade. We believe that promotion and implementation of these measures by all will contribute to greater participation in world trade, thus allowing the creation of new international trade flows. Trade efficiency measures would also result in reduction of trade transaction costs by a quarter or by up to 100 billion dollars annually by the year 2000. We shall strive to reach these objectives through national and collective efforts.

Trade efficiency measures

9. To achieve these goals, we have decided to initiate a worldwide process to enhance participation in international trade through a set of practical actions, recommendations and guidelines which may be adopted by Governments, international and national organizations and enterprises as appropriate. These recommendations and guidelines address six areas in which we believe immediate action is feasible and likely to generate tangible results for international trade: customs, transport, banking and insurance, information for trade, business prac-

tices, and telecommunications. As a first step in this direction, we are officially launching the Trade Point Global Network, which will allow all member countries to trade more efficiently with each other and help those who have so far remained at the fringe of international trade to participate actively and profitably in it, in particular the least developed countries and small and medium-sized enterprises in all countries.

10. Trade efficiency is a priority area for Governments, international and national organizations and enterprises, all of which will have important and complementary roles to play in the implementation and follow-up of these recommendations and guidelines. Areas of particular importance in which their energies will need to be combined are those of the adoption, promotion and implementation of international standards, as well as technical and legal frameworks facilitating trade-efficient measures.

11. We agree that technical assistance programmes in the following areas deserve immediate attention: training and awareness in the main areas of trade facilitation and trade efficiency; integration of trade-efficient measures in customs and in financial, transportation, and telecommunications sectors; and promotion and use of agreed international norms and standards for collecting and transmitting trade-related information and messages. We therefore invite the international community to provide substantial and rapid technical and financial assistance to developing countries and countries in transition for the establishment and internetworking of trade points, as well as the implementation of the recommendations and guidelines identified above. The specific needs of the least developed countries in these areas should be considered as a priority.

Role of UNCTAD in promoting trade efficiency

12. We designate UNCTAD as the focal point in the implementation of the present Declaration, which will require coordinated efforts by many national and international bodies, with the United Nations system having a central and irreplaceable role. We commend the close cooperation already established between UNCTAD and other bodies, notably the United Nations Economic Commission for Europe (ECE), the International Trade Centre (ITC), the Customs Cooperation Council (CCC) and the United Nations Economic and Social Commission for Asia and the Pacific (ESCAP). We urge that these efforts continue in an integrated fashion, generating synergies among all organizations carrying out this highly valuable work. Coordination with the GATT/WTO and all United Nations regional economic commissions will be of particular importance in facilitation of trade.

13. We note that the rapid transition in technology will bring changes to the present solutions in the years to come. We therefore consider it necessary that policy issues related to trade efficiency continue to be explored by UNCTAD, in close cooperation with other relevant organizations. We encourage UNCTAD to continue its programmes supporting the implementation of efficient trade measures and the extension of trade points to all countries. We look forward to increased trade through more efficient trade.

Appendix

RECOMMENDATIONS AND GUIDELINES
FOR TRADE EFFICIENCY

RECOMMENDATIONS TO GOVERNMENTS

A. Banking and insurance

The availability of modern trade-related finance, payment and risk management products is a critical element in the expansion of international trade within the developing world. Trade inefficiency in financial services can have a significant impact on the ability of firms, particularly small and medium-size enterprises (SMEs), to participate in international trade or to compete effectively with exporters from other countries.

The development of efficient markets for financial services will facilitate increased international trade in goods and services through improvements in the products and levels of service provided by the trade finance community. To further the capacity, efficiency, competitiveness and general development of their financial services industry, consistent with the progress of the General Agreement on Trade in Services negotiations, Governments may consider, bearing in mind their prevailing national circumstances:

1. Addressing the structural aspects of the market for trade-related financial services when formulating policy in the area of financial services regulation. Policy-makers should consider the direct and indirect economic impact of restrictions affecting trade-related financial services, particularly their effect on trading enterprises' competitiveness;

2. Reviewing their current laws and regulations affecting trade finance, insurance and international payments to ensure that they are consistent with accepted international practices;

3. Ratifying and implementing existing international conventions which seek to further harmonize international trade finance law;

4. Evaluating existing exchange control regulations to ensure that they facilitate the use of current financing and payment techniques;

5. Allowing trading enterprises to secure foreign exchange to purchase modern financial products which enhance their competitiveness.

B. Customs

Customs play a key role in international trade. Every international trade transaction involves at least two Customs interventions, one at export and one at import. It is clear, therefore, that the manner in which Customs conduct their business has a substantial impact on the movement of goods across international borders. To promote the efficient flow of goods in international trade, Governments, through their Customs authorities, should:

1. In consultation with other interested parties (both governmental and non-governmental, as appropriate), clearly define their corporate objectives for Customs and develop and publish an overall long-term plan which sets out the manner in which it is intended to achieve these objectives;

2. Urgently examine their existing customs practices and institute a programme of reform for those procedures that are identified as inefficient or redundant. Reference should be made to existing international conventions on Customs process simplification and harmonization (the Kyoto Convention of the Customs Cooperation Council). This should be undertaken with national trade and transport interests to ensure full coordination of carrier, port and Customs controls;

3. Maximize the use of information technology to assist Customs in the efficient performance of their duties. Computer applications for the Customs processing of commercial and financial transactions should be developed taking into consideration the experiences of all countries. Consideration should be given where applicable to implementing UNCTAD's programme "for Customs computerization and reform, the Automated System for Customs Data (ASYCUDA). Computer interfaces (aimed at using United Nations EDIFACT interchange standards) which allow for the electronic submission of manifests, goods declarations, etc., should be developed and made available to traders;

4. Ensure the effective use of scarce manpower resources by means of risk assessment, profiling, selectivity and targeting techniques to identify high-risk consignments for physical examination. The proportion of consignments to be physically examined by Customs should be kept to a minimum consistent with the accomplishment of control objectives;

5. Take steps to make available facilities for pre-arrival processing of transactions, which can deliver significant trade facilitation benefits and, with appropriate safeguards, does not compromise in any way the control objectives of Customs. The electronic submission of pre-arrival cargo data further facilitates this process;

6. Examine closely the possibility of speeding up, as much as possible, the process of goods release based on a minimum of essential information. However, they should ensure that all information necessary for proper revenue collection, accounting, and precise statistical reporting is communicated to the Customs authorities;

7. Rationalize the cargo clearance process, which frequently requires the intervention of several government agencies in addition to Customs, through coordinated interventions by the agencies concerned or by investing responsibility for all cargo clearance activities in one single authority, i.e. Customs;

8. Simplify procedures for determining customs value, which can cause significant delays in the clearance of import consignments, through the use of the Customs valuation method prescribed in the GATT Agreement, as administered by the Customs Cooperation Council, which is administratively less complex than other methods currently in use in some countries;

9. Endeavour, where possible and when high Customs tariffs are developed for national revenue, to broaden their tax base so that Customs tariffs may be moder-

ated, since excessively high Customs tariffs encourage evasion through a variety of fraudulent practices and make enforcement more difficult;

10. Take steps to foster a cooperative rather than a confrontational approach to Customs operations. The Memorandum of Understanding (MOU) programme of the Customs Cooperation Council should be used as a vehicle for greater cooperation between Customs authorities and commercial operators;

11. Take steps to ensure the highest level of integrity and professional standards within their Customs service. The measures identified by the Customs Cooperation Council in the Arusha Declaration on Integrity in Customs should be implemented. Effective measures are also required to discourage low standards of integrity in the trading community;

12. Institute Customs reform programmes aimed at enhancing the efficiency and effectiveness of their Customs services, thereby avoiding as far as possible, for example, the need to use the services of pre-shipment inspection agencies to carry out Customs-related activities. While recourse to such services might be a necessity in certain circumstances, it should be regarded as an interim measure and conducted in conformity with the provisions of the agreement on preshipment inspection (PSI) annexed to the Marrakesh agreement;

13. Consider, as appropriate, setting minimum standards for shipping agents, freight forwarders and Customs clearing agents/brokers or encourage these professions to set their own standards and monitor performance, since the factors causing delays in the release of goods include inefficiency and lack of professionalism on the part of some members of these professions;

14. Ensure maximum transparency and fluidity of Customs operations by providing the trading community with the necessary information on Customs formalities and requirements. Such information should be kept up to date and should be easily accessible;

15. Enhance Customs controls and facilitate import clearance by considering, on a bilateral (or multilateral) basis, the routine electronic transmission of export data from the country of export to the Customs authority of the importing country, in accordance with the laws and regulations concerning disclosure of information;

16. Ensure, in countries where foreign trade statistics are based on Customs data, the reliability of the raw statistical data, as well as their timely transfer to the institutions responsible for the compilation of trade statistics;

17. Ensure that Customs are adequately resourced to perform their designated role efficiently, effectively and to a high standard of professional ethics, since a Customs service starved of resources will certainly be an obstacle to trade;

18. Offer training (including through scholarships) especially directed to Customs professionals in developing countries for training nationally or abroad in cooperation with the Customs Cooperation Council (CCC) and/or UNCTAD. This training should cover the requirements of international Customs conventions and regional integration, with emphasis on operational aspects;

19. Ensure, through their representatives on the ruling body of the Customs Cooperation Council, that the Council is adequately resourced to carry out the urgent technical assistance tasks which it is called upon to do. The Council, as the inter-

national organization for Customs matters, has a key role to play with regard to the implementation of many of the above recommendations by its member administrations.

C. Business information for trade

Business information plays a key role in international marketing and competitiveness. Access to timely, accurate business information and the ability to use the information is a major factor in international trade efficiency. To promote the free flow of business information and equal access to that information by enterprises of all sizes, Governments should:

1. Encourage enterprises, in particular newcomers to international trade and small and medium-size enterprises, to explore the scope for internationalization, as appropriate;

2. Facilitate circulation of, and access to, sources of economic and business information, which represent an important input in the transition to a more outward-looking development pattern. Particular consideration should be given to SMEs and newcomers to international trade. For example, trade promotion organizations and trade commissioner services could be used. International experience on the conditions of success for running efficient business centres and services should be taken into account;

3. Improve training capacities for more effective use of business information, particularly in developing countries and economies in transition. This should include the strengthening of local training institutions (training of trainers), as well as specialized training assistance to trade promotion institutions, business associations and the enterprise sector;

4. Make special efforts to ensure that the necessary telecommunications infrastructures are in place to permit effective access to business information sources, such as on-line databases, especially in developing countries and countries in transition;

5. Support the use of internationally accepted standards, formats, and coding systems when used in the dissemination of information;

6. Ensure a non-discriminatory and conducive policy framework for commercial suppliers of business information;

7. Ensure that a focal point exists in each country to collect, process and make available for retrieval all relevant information on the country's trade regulations, product by product and using standard formats;

8. Develop a coordinated approach to the complex tasks of government institutions relating to business information, for example by establishing a national focal point;

9. Ensure the availability and reliability of up-to-date trade statistics, including those on trade volume and values, using internationally compatible nomenclatures; submit those statistics on a timely basis to the United Nations Statistical Office; and encourage the use of available modern technologies in the collection and dissemination of statistics;

10. Encourage public and private business information services to strengthen their capacities as intermediaries and interpreters of business information, in particular for small and medium-size enterprises;

11. Encourage government departments which generate business information, such as departments of statistics, Customs, ministries of trade, central banks, etc., to develop efficient methods of disseminating that data to meet the needs of national and international business communities;

12. Encourage trade points to provide national and international business information.

D. Transport

Trade and transport are inextricably linked; efficient transport services are a prerequisite for successful trading. Growth in international trade demands the implementation of trade efficiency measures in the transport sector. To support rapid growth in international trade, Governments should:

1. Review current transport laws and regulations with a view to encouraging the adoption of commercial practices in the transport chain and investment by both domestic and foreign investors;

2. Implement specific transport operations improvements, such as encouraging the development of multimodal transport operations, the formation of block-train services, and granting of container terminal concessions to companies that operate according to commercial practices; provide guidelines to update commercial banking and insurance practices in line with international practices recommended by the International Chamber of Commerce (ICC); and stimulate private investment in training;

3. Develop subregional cooperation projects regarding harmonization of transport regulatory policies and legal regimes to find multilateral solutions to existing problems, particularly in the field of Customs transit, taking into account international models of aligned documentation developed by the Customs Cooperation Council and UNCTAD;

4. Encourage the establishment of subregional databases on transport.

E. Telecommunications

Telecommunications are a key factor for international trade in goods and services. Open access to international telecommunications is critical for efficient trade, and therefore Governments should:

1. Develop efficient telecommunications services to serve the needs of participants in international trade;

2. Prepare for and allow competition with regard to value-added services as appropriate;

3. Identify the minimum service requirements necessary for the efficient use of telecommunications networks for local, national and international trade by small and medium-sized enterprises;

4. Provide the necessary support and assistance to enhance capacity-building in the area of telecommunications in order to allow all participants in international trade to benefit from efficient trade practices and trade-supporting services. In doing so, they

should keep in mind the Buenos Aires Declaration and Action Plan adopted at the First World Telecommunications Development Conference in March 1994. Special attention should be granted to the specific situation of the least developed countries;

5. Ensure development of network access in remote or low-density regions for small business users through the adoption of appropriate network architectures;

6. Establish the necessary telecommunications networks and services to enable the efficient functioning and interconnecting of all trade points, thereby achieving maximum benefits for all participants.

F. Business practices

Obtaining new market opportunities requires not only the maintenance of free trade principles, but also substantial improvements in the efficiency of the overall trading process. Trade efficiency can be achieved as a result of trade facilitation, improving access to better marketing information and the adoption of new business concepts. In this context, Governments should:

1. Ensure that trade facilitation issues are taken into account when formulating trade and transport policies;

2. Set up national committees where government services and commercial operators are represented to promote trade facilitation where not already in existence, with a clear remit:

   —To reduce administrative impediments, in both public and private sectors, and search for concerted solutions to international trade- and transport-related issues;

   —To encourage the use of best practice, including information technology, throughout the trading, transport and distribution, and payment processes, following international standards; and

   —To help develop the skills of the people involved;

3. Encourage subregional meetings of national trade facilitation committees;

4. Ensure that the national trade facilitation committee assists traders in carrying out their work in two ways:

   —Simplifying, coordinating and standardizing procedures for exports and imports by all modes of transport;

   —Developing an aligned import and export document system, both for paper documents and their electronic equivalent, based on international standards, the United Nations Layout Key for paper documents, and the United Nations Electronic Data Interchange for Administration, Commerce and Transport (EDIFACT);

5. Encourage close cooperation among all organizations working in the area of business practices, especially the continuing close cooperation among UNCTAD, the Economic Commission for Europe (ECE) and the International Trade Centre UNCTAD/GATT;

6. Establish transparent and simplified procedures to obtain licences for exports or imports of restricted or sensitive products. Once a licence is issued, control should be linked to routine export and import controls, for example, customs clearance;

7. Establish simplified procedures to obtain foreign exchange for international trade;

8. Simplify the procedures for certification of origin;

9. Ensure that national regulations on dangerous goods conform to the relevant international standards; where possible, the dangerous goods declaration should be incorporated in an existing commercial document;

10. Review their international trade statistical needs in order to keep data requirements to a minimum. Data should be collected at a time, and in a way, that cause minimum delay to the movement of goods, such as periodic scheduled returns;

11. Ensure, when the public sector provides international trade services or buys and sells goods, that efficient procedures are used.

RECOMMENDATIONS TO TRADE POINTS

Trade Points are a valuable source of full, impartial and accurate information on all aspects of trade transactions. They seek to supply the best possible information in all areas of trade, guaranteeing equal treatment to all their partners and actively avoiding any monopoly or exclusive position in relation to service providers and other trade points. They assist traders in carrying out trade transactions, using modern information technology and in accordance with international standards. In addition, they are laboratories for national trade efficiency policies.

The two main goals of Trade Points in assisting their national exporters and importers are to lower the cost of trade transactions and to encourage expanded participation in international trade, especially the participation of small and medium-sized enterprises.

The successful completion of the Uruguay Round has opened new opportunities for international trade. Trade Points can provide a valuable service by advising their clients on how to take advantage of these new opportunities.

A. Banking and insurance

Trade Points should:

1. Provide export clients, particularly SMEs, with comprehensive financial advisory services, including information on available finance, payment and risk management alternatives;

2. Establish a computerized database of qualified financial services providers to support financial advisory services;

3. Develop as soon as possible a database for providers of financing, payment services, credit insurance and credit information;

4. Facilitate access to foreign credit information;

5. Be prepared to advise clients on the pre-shipment financing facilities available in their country or region;

6. Facilitate access to export factoring services for their export clients;

7. Be able to refer clients to qualified forfeiters and assist client importers in obtaining the requisite guarantees;

8. Be able to refer clients to qualified countertrade brokers and financial institutions which specialize in facilitating countertrade transactions;

9. Determine the potential demand for lease financing services based upon the local volume of capital equipment exports. Local financial institutions with a leasing capability or international leasing specialists should be included in the financial services referral service;

10. Facilitate the availability of information on credit insurance to their clients;

11. Provide advice to exporters, in particular new exporters, for adequate use of credit insurance in light of the method of payment of the commercial transaction and potential risk;

12. Work cooperatively with national and multilateral agencies to draw up finance and guarantee programmes which are appropriate to their clients' needs and the capabilities of domestic financial systems;

13. Through the Trade Point Network, seek to participate in national and regional efforts, both public and private, to develop or improve payment and clearing systems. In these efforts, electronic data interchange (EDT) capabilities should be designed under Electronic Data Interchange for Administration, Commerce and Transport (EDIFACT) standards, and the system design should facilitate linkages to other national and regional clearing systems.

B. Telecommunications

Trade Points should:

1. Equip themselves initially with the basic telecommunications equipment necessary to service their clients and link up with other Trade Points. This basic equipment should include capacity for EDT, E-mail and database services, and all functions should be based on the use of appropriate international standards. The level of equipment should be in keeping with each Trade Point's service management capacity and with available human and financial resources, but Trade Points should seek to enhance their capacity to match the growing needs of clients;

2. Develop interconnections through networks of all types so that they are able to contact a wide range of markets for their clients. In developing countries, where telecommunications resources may not be sufficient initially to provide the level of services desired by their clients, development of telecommunications capacity should be a priority;

3. Encourage training in the use of communication and information technology for trade to increase capacities within their own countries;

4. Create, in cooperation with other Trade Points in the UNCTAD Trade Point Global Network, a mechanism to allow easy and direct transfer of materials and technical assistance from private sector donors to Trade Points requesting such assistance, particularly Trade Points in LDCs. This mechanism, in conjunction with UNCTAD, should seek *inter alia* to obtain access and preferential terms to international telecommunication services.

GUIDELINES FOR OTHER PARTICIPANTS
IN INTERNATIONAL TRADE

A. Business practices

Guidelines for traders

International Trade is more complex in many ways than domestic trade. Firstly, there are more parties (often 12-15) and therefore more documents; secondly, the delivery of the goods can be made not only at the factory or customers' gates but at 11 other points (e.g. ports, frontiers) in between. This means that the division of costs, risks and responsibilities between the buyer and the seller varies depending on the terms used. For a smooth and effective transaction, it is necessary for the seller to deliver the goods at the right place and time and for the buyer to complete the movement of the goods and pay for them, as per contract.

When preparing to trade internationally it is important, therefore, for all companies, large and small, to develop a trading strategy and plan operations carefully.

Traders should:

1. Prepare a suitable export strategy which covers:
   —Market research;
   —Arranging the contract;
   —Getting the goods to market;
   —Documentation and export administration;
   —Getting paid; and
   —Customer service;

2. Concentrate, in market research, on only a few markets with sufficient potential and where the product has also some competitive advantage; ensure that all costs are identified and are included in the sale price; prepare a marketing plan that allocates adequate resources;

3. Ensure that the correct terms of trade and payment are used in arranging the contract; train staff to use INCOTERMS 1990, produced by the International Chamber of Commerce; investigate payment options, including comparative cost and risks;

4. Use a carefully chosen freight forwarder, or export administration company, who can obtain competitive quotations for their products and can arrange transport, insurance, official documentation and customs clearance, for all methods except post;

5. Follow international documents standards and the national aligned document system; install a system compatible with requirements; pay particular attention to providing accurate, timely information to customers, Customs and other official bodies and to all those providing services, e.g. forwarders, ports, carriers, and banks;

6. Plan and manage the export payment process, selecting the most appropriate payment methods; when using letters of credit, bearing in mind the high risk of mistakes and errors, etc., and the potential payment delays that stem from them:

—Send a pro-form to the buyer at an early stage;

—Check credits for accuracy as soon as they are received, and have them corrected.

7. Importers should use the most appropriate purchasing practices to ensure that the goods can be cleared of Customs, etc., as soon as they arrive.

Guidelines for providers of international trade services

1. International trade services should:

   Simplify the procedures associated with their services as far as possible and use international standard practices and information standards for documents and electronic messages.

2. Transport services should:

   Develop multi-purpose shipping notes and consignment instructions as part of national document systems;

   Revise commercial and official practices as countries develop multimodal transport systems.

3. Maritime operators should:

   Offer traders non-negotiable documents as an alternative to negotiable bills of lading.

4. Financial services should:

   Review commercial payment procedures associated with letters of credit and documentary collections to ensure that they follow current trade/transport practices and international standards;

   Introduce and encourage express money transfer systems, which reduce payment "float time" to the minimum;

   Simplify cargo insurance procedures, using the "open cover" principle whenever possible.

5. Communications services should:

   Interconnect value added networks (VANs), so that traders can contact all their customers/suppliers. VANs should provide levels of security and end-to-end audit to meet user requirements.

B. Business information for trade

1. All suppliers of business information are encouraged to prepare in a timely fashion and improve business information for and about developing countries and economies in transition, in particular in the area of company information.

2. Suppliers of business information in developed countries are invited to provide business information to small and medium-sized enterprises of developing countries on a preferential basis whenever possible.

3. All participants in international trade are encouraged to strengthen training capacities for more effective use of business information.

4. Suppliers and users of business information are encouraged to use existing standards and coding systems, e.g. Electronic Data Interchange for Administration,

Commerce and Transport (EDIFACT) for data interchange, Company Register (COMREG) for company registers, and the Harmonized System (HS) for product classification.

5. Business associations are encouraged to strengthen the important contribution that they are making towards increasing the efficiency of international marketing through business information. In line with their specific mandates and resources, they are urged to increase assistance and training on how to interpret and apply business information effectively for export and import marketing. Business associations are urged to expand the services available to small and medium-sized enterprises (SMEs) and newcomers to international trade by facilitating membership arrangements. In this process, particular attention should be given to the needs of firms in developing countries. Conversely, SMEs are urged to join local business associations to strengthen them and to help them meet the particular needs of SMEs.

6. Regional and international organizations are encouraged to adopt pricing policies for foreign trade and other business statistics so that this information is affordable to all potential users, so as to encourage new participants to enter global markets, particularly from developing countries and countries in transition.

Chapter II

PROCEDURAL AND ORGANIZATIONAL MATTERS

A. Senior Officials Segment

1. Opening of the Segment

1. The Senior Officials Segment of the United Nations International Symposium on Trade Efficiency was opened on Monday, 17 October 1994, by Ms. S. Shelton (United States of America), Chairperson of the Preparatory Committee for the United Nations International Symposium for Trade Efficiency.

2. Opening addresses were delivered by Ms. M. Kimble, Chairperson of the Senior Officials Segment; Mr. D. Bennett, Assistant Secretary of State for International Organization Affairs, United States of America; Mr. G. Lashutka, Mayor of Columbus; Mr. C. Fortin, Officer-in-Charge of UNCTAD; and Mr. R. Butler (Australia), President of the Economic and Social Council.

2. Election of officers

(Agenda item 1)

3. At their opening meeting, the Senior Officials elected their officers by acclamation, as follows:

Chairperson:	Ms. M. Kimble	(United States of America)
Vice-Chairmen:	Mr. W. Rossier	(Switzerland)
	Mr. A. von Hardenberg	(Germany)
	Mrs. J. Wright	(United Kingdom)

	Mr. Y. Afanassiev	(Russian Federation)
	Mr. T. Husak	(Czech Republic)
	Mr. T. Roy	(India)
	Mr. A. A. Khan	(Bangladesh)
	Mr. E. Tironi	(Chile)
	Mr. M. A. Becerra	(Bolivia)
	Mr. D. du Rand	(South Africa)
Rapporteur:	Mr. A. Rachdi	(Morocco)

4. The Senior Officials also decided to recommend that the country composition of the Bureau would remain the same for the Ministerial Segment.

3. Adoption of the rules of procedure

(Agenda item 2)

5. The Senior Officials decided that the rules of procedure of the Symposium would be, *mutatis mutandis*, those of the Trade and Development Board.

4. Adoption of the agenda and organization of work

(Agenda item 3)

6. The Senior Officials adopted their provisional agenda (TD/SYMP.TE/1), as follows:

1. Election of officers

2. Adoption of the rules of procedure

3. Adoption of the agenda and organization of work

4. Report of the Preparatory Committee

5. Consideration of the draft Columbus Ministerial Declaration

6. Consideration of draft recommendations and guidelines for trade efficiency

7. Facilitating global trade

8. Presentation of solutions for key sectors of trade efficiency: Customs, business information for trade, banking and insurance, transport, telecommunications, business practices

9. Provisional agenda for the Ministerial Segment

10. Other business

11. Adoption of the report of the Senior Officials Segment to the Ministerial Segment.

7. With regard to the organization of work, the Senior Officials decided that agenda items 5 and 6 would be taken up in the Bureau and that the Bureau would recommend to the Senior Officials in plenary the transmission of the draft Columbus Ministerial Declaration and of the draft recommendations and guidelines for trade to the Ministerial Segment for adoption.

8. Concerning agenda item 7, the Senior Officials decided that it would be taken up in a special segment. The keynote speaker for the special segment was Mr. R. Walker, Simpler Trade Procedures Board, United Kingdom.

9. Concerning agenda item 8, the Senior Officials decided that six sectoral sessions would be held with the participation of key actors and experts in the sectors. Each session would have a Chairman and a Session Leader, as follows: Customs: Mr. G. Ludlow, Comptroller of Customs, New Zealand (Chairman) and Mr. J. Shaver, Secretary-General, World Customs Organization (Session Leader); trade information: Mr. W. Rossier (Switzerland), Vice-Chairman of the Senior Officials Segment (Chairman) and Mr. J. D. Belisle, Executive Director, International Trade Centre UNCTAD/GATT (Session Leader); banking and insurance: Mr. A. A. Khan, Chairman of the National Revenue Board, Bangladesh (Chairman) and Mr. K. Ouedraogo, Vice-Governor, Central Bank of West African States, Senegal; transport: Mr. A. Brahimi, Director-General of Foreign Trade, Algeria (Chairman) and Mr. K. Hannarskjöld, CEO and President, Atwater Institute, Canada (Session Leader); telecommunications: Mr. E. Tironi (Chile), Vice-Chairman of the Senior Officials Segment (Chairman) and Mr. J. Arlandis, Director, Institut de l'Audiovisuel et des Télécommunications en Europe, France, and Mr. L. Gille, CEO, Sirius, France (Session Leaders); business practices: Mr. T. Blomfeldt (Finland), Chairman of ECE WP.4 (Chairman *cum* Session Leader).

10. Finally, the Senior Officials agreed that the regional coordinators and China, as well as the five Chairmen of the Sectoral sessions, should be fully associated with the work of the Bureau.

5. Report of the Preparatory Committee

(Agenda item 4)

11. The Chairperson of the Preparatory Committee made a statement in introduction to the Preparatory Committee's report (TD/SYMP.TE/4).

6. Consideration of the draft Columbus Ministerial Declaration and the draft recommendations and guidelines for trade efficiency

(Agenda items 5 and 6)

12. At their closing plenary, on 18 October 1994, the Senior Officials recommended to the Ministerial Segment the adoption of the draft Columbus Ministerial Declaration (TD/SYMP.TE/R.1) and the draft recommendations and guidelines referred to therein (TD/SYMP.TE/R.2).

7. Presentation of solutions for key sectors of trade efficiency: Customs, business information for trade, banking and insurance, transport, telecommunications, business practices

(Agenda item 8)

13. The Senior Officials decided that the Chairman's summary of the work of the sectoral sessions on policy issues and possible actions for further consideration (TD/SYMP.TE/Misc.2/Rev. 1) should be transmitted to the Ministers for consideration in their discussions and deliberations during the substantive segments.

8. Provisional agenda for the Ministerial Segment

(Agenda item 9)

14. At their closing plenary, on 18 October 1994, the Senior Officials approved the provisional agenda for the Ministerial Segment (TD/SYMP.TE/1/Add.1/Rev.1).

9. Adoption of the report of the Senior Officials Segment to the Ministerial Segment

(Agenda item 11)

15. The Senior Officials agreed that the procedural part of their report would be completed by the Rapporteur under the authority of the Chairperson and would constitute part of the records of the symposium.

B. Ministerial Segment

1. Election of the President and opening of the Ministerial Segment

(Agenda item 1)

16. The Ministerial Segment of the United Nations International Symposium on Trade Efficiency was opened on Wednesday, 19 October 1994, by Ms. M. Kimble (United States of America), Chairperson of the Senior Officials Segment.

17. Mr. Ron Brown, Secretary of Commerce, United States of America, was elected President of the Ministerial Segment by acclamation.

2. Election of the other members of the Bureau

(Agenda item 2)

18. At its opening meeting, the Ministerial Segment elected the other members of the Bureau as follows:

Vice-Presidents:	Mr. F. Blankart	(Switzerland)
	Mr. E. A. Horig	(Germany)
	Sir Derek Hornby	(United Kingdom)
	Mr. G. Gabounia	(Russian Federation)
	Mr. V. Dlouhy	(Czech Republic)
	Mr. P. Mukherjee	(India)
	Mr. M. Shamsul Islam	(Bangladesh)
	Mr. C. Mladinic	(Chile)
	Mr. T. A. Manuel	(South Africa)
	Mr. C. Morales Landivar	(Bolivia)
Rapporteur-General:	Mr. O. Kabbaj	(Morocco)

3. Adoption of the agenda and organization of work

(Agenda item 3)

19. The Ministerial Segment adopted its provisional agenda (TD/SYMP.TE/1/Add.1/ Rev.1), as follows:

    1. Election of the President and opening of the Ministerial Segment

    2. Election of the other members of the Bureau

    3. Adoption of the agenda and organization of work

    4. Report of the Senior Officials Segment

    5. Adoption of the Columbus Ministerial Declaration on Trade Efficiency and launching of the Trade Point Global Network

    6. A vision for international trade:

       (a) Truly global trade

       (b) Technology and trade

       (c) Role of Governments

       (d) Trade efficiency and development

    7. Other business

    8. Closing of the Symposium

20. The Ministerial Segment also approved the organization of work as set out in document TD/SYMP.TE/1/Add.1/Rev.1.

4. Report of the Senior Officials Segment

(Agenda item 4)

21. The Chairperson of the Senior Officials Segment made a statement reporting on the work of the Senior Officials.

5. Adoption of the Columbus Ministerial Declaration on Trade Efficiency and launching of the Trade Point Global Network

(Agenda item 5)

22. At its opening plenary meeting, on 19 October 1994, the Ministerial Segment adopted the Columbus Ministerial Declaration on Trade Efficiency (see part I above). At its closing plenary meeting, on 21 October 1994, the Ministerial Segment decided to transmit the Columbus Ministerial Declaration on Trade Efficiency and the supporting recommendations and guidelines for trade efficiency to the General Assembly.

6. Addresses delivered at the inaugural ceremony and opening plenary, and message received

23. At the inaugural ceremony, addresses were delivered by Mr. Boutros Boutros-Ghali, Secretary-General of the United Nations; Mr. Greg Lashutka, Mayor of

Columbus; Mr. George Voinovich, Governor of Ohio; Mr. Ron Brown, President of the Symposium.

24. At the opening plenary, addresses were delivered by Mr. Carlos Fortin, Officer-in-Charge of UNCTAD; Mr. Ron Brown, President of the Symposium; Senator John Glenn, United States of America, on behalf of the host country; Mr. Shamsul Islam, Bangladesh, on behalf of the least developed countries; Mr. Supachai Panitchpakdi, Thailand; Mr. Ernest-August Horig, Germany, and Mr. A. van Agt, European Commission, jointly on behalf of the European Union by the Presidency and the Commission of the European Union; and Mr. Alan Winters, World Bank.

25. A message was received from Mr. Victor Chernomyrdin, Prime Minister of the Russian Federation (TD/SYMP.TE/5).

7. A vision for international trade: (a) truly global trade; (b) technology and trade; (c) role of Governments; (d) trade efficiency and development

(Agenda item 6)

26. In accordance with the approved organization of work, each sub-item was introduced through a panel discussion led by a moderator, followed by comments from participating ministers. The moderators for the respective sub-items were; truly global trade: Mr. Guy de Jonquières, Business Editor, The Financial Times; technology and trade: Mr. Denis Gilhooly, Publishing Director, Communications Week International; role of Governments: Mr. Guy de Jonquières, Business Editor, The Financial Times; trade efficiency and development: Mr. Lou Dobbs, Senior Vice-President, CNN. Under sub-item (d), a global Trade Point video conference involving several Trade Points took place.

27. At the closing plenary, on 21 October 1994, the President presented a draft summary of issues discussed during the plenary meetings of the Ministerial Segment.

28. The Ministerial Segment noted the summaries presented by the President of the Ministerial Segment and the Chairperson of the Senior Officials Segment and decided to transmit them to the Trade and Development Board and to request the Trade and Development Board to report thereon to the General Assembly. (For the text of the summaries, see document TD/B/EX(8)/2 - TD/SYMP.TE/7).

8. Advisory Board and Honorary Board

29. In accordance with a decision taken by the Ad Hoc Working Group on Trade Efficiency at its second session (15–19 November 1993), the Executive Secretary set up an Advisory Board composed of internationally known personalities with a record of innovativeness and efficiency and an interest in international trade to contribute in their personal capacity to enriching and introducing some of the subject matters to be dealt with in the Ministerial Segment of the Symposium (TD/B/40(2)/3, annex II, para.7).

30. The Advisory Board was constituted as follows: Mr. Hrant Bagratian, Prime Minister, Armenia; Mr. Carlo De Benedetti, Chairman and CEO, Olivetti S.p.A.; Mr. Richard Butler, President of the Economic and Social Council; Ms. Liliana Canale,

Minister of Industry, Tourism, Integration and International Trade Negotiations, Peru; Mr. Jean-Pascal Delamuraz, Federal Councillor, Switzerland; Mr. Vladimir Dlouhy, Minister of Industry and Trade, Czech Republic; Mr. Kablan D. Duncan, Prime Minister, Côte d'Ivoire; Mr. Manuel Feliú, President of CEAL, Chile; Mr. Christopher Galvin, COO Motorola; Mr. Florin Georgescu, State Minister, Minister of Finance, Romania; Ms. Rima Khalaf, Minister of Trade and Industry, Jordan; Mr. Trevor A. Manuel, Minister of Trade and Industry, South Africa; Mr. Jean Monty, President and CEO, Northern Telecom, Canada; Mr. Shri Pranab Mukherjee, Union Minister for Commerce, India; Mr. Rubens Ricupero, Former Minister of Finance, Brazil.

31. In addition to the Advisory Board, an Honorary Board was set up, constituted as follows: Mr. Rafeeuddin Ahmed, Executive Secretary, ESCAP; Mr. Sabah Bakjaji, Executive Secretary, ESCWA; Mr. Yves Berthelot, Executive Secretary, ECE; Mr. Michel Camdessus, Managing Director, International Monetary Fund; Mr. Osama J. I. Faquih, President, Islamic Development Bank; Mr. Enrique V. Iglesias, President, Inter-American Development Bank; Mr. Mauricio de María y Campos, Director-General, UNIDO; Mr. Babacar Ndiaye, President and CEO, African Development Bank; Mr. Lewis T. Preston, President, World Bank; Mr. Gert Rosenthal, Executive Secretary, ECLAC; Mr. James G. Speth, Administrator, UNDP; Mr. Peter D. Sutherland, Director-General, GATT; Mr. Pekka Tarjanne, Director-General, ITU; Mr. Layashi Yaker, Executive Secretary, ECA; Mr. Carlos Fortin, Officer-in-Charge, UNCTAD; Mr. Denis Belisle, Executive Director, International Trade Centre, UNCTAD/GATT; Mr. James W. Shaver, Secretary-General, Customs Cooperation Council.

9. Attendance

32. The following States, members of UNCTAD, were represented at the United Nations International Symposium on Trade Efficiency: Albania; Algeria; Angola; Argentina; Armenia; Australia; Austria; Azerbaijan; Bahamas; Bangladesh; Belarus; Belgium; Belize; Benin; Bhutan; Bolivia; Botswana; Brazil; Brunei Darussalam; Bulgaria; Burkina Faso; Burundi; Cameroon; Canada; Cape Verde; Central African Republic; Chad; Chile; China; Colombia; Comoros; Costa Rica; Côte d'Ivoire; Croatia; Cuba; Czech Republic; Denmark; Dubouti; Dominican Republic; Ecuador; Egypt; El Salvador; Eritrea; Estonia; Ethiopia; Finland; France; Gabon; Georgia; Germany; Ghana; Greece; Guinea; Guyana; Honduras; Hungary; India; Indonesia; Iran (Islamic Republic of); Iraq; Israel; Italy; Jamaica; Japan; Jordan; Kenya; Kuwait; Kyrgyzstan; Lesotho; Liberia; Libyan Arab Jamahiriya; Lithuania; Madagascar; Malawi; Maldives; Mali; Malta; Marshall Islands; Mauritania; Mauritius; Mexico; Mongolia; Morocco; Mozambique; Myanmar; Namibia; Nepal; Netherlands; New Zealand; Nicaragua; Niger; Nigeria; Norway; Oman; Paraguay; Peru; Philippines; Poland; Portugal; Qatar; Republic of Korea; Republic of Moldova; Romania; Russian Federation; Saint Vincent and the Grenadines; San Marino; Sao Tome and Principe; Saudi Arabia; Senegal; Sierra Leone; Singapore; Slovakia; Slovenia; Solomon Islands; South Africa; Spain; Sri Lanka; Sudan; Suriname; Sweden; Switzerland; Thailand; Togo; Tonga; Tunisia; Turkey; Uganda; Ukraine; United Arab Emirates; United Kingdom of Great Britain and Northern Ireland; United Republic of Tanzania; United States of America; Uruguay; Viet Nam; Yemen; Zambia; Zimbabwe.

33. The Economic Commission for Europe, the Economic Commission for Africa, and the United Nations Development Programme were represented at the Symposium. The International Trade Centre UNCTAD/GATT was also represented.

34. The following specialized agencies were represented at the Symposium: World Bank, United Nations Industrial Development Organization.

35. The following intergovernmental organizations were represented at the Symposium: African Development Bank; Commonwealth Secretariat; Customs Cooperation Council; European Community; League of Arab States; Organization of the Islamic Conference.

36. The following non-governmental organizations were represented at the Symposium:

    General Category

    General Union of Chambers of Commerce, Industry and Agriculture of Arab States; International Chamber of Commerce; World Federation of United Nations Associations.

    Special Category

    EDI World Institute; Federation of African National Insurance Companies.

37. The following invited organization participated in the Symposium: South Investment, Trade and Technology Data Exchange Centre.

10. Motion of thanks to the host country and host city

38. At the closing plenary, on 21 October 1994, the representative of Switzerland moved a motion of thanks to the City of Columbus, the State of Ohio, and the United States.

11. Closure of the Symposium

39. Closing statements were made by Mr. Ron Brown, President of the Symposium; Mr. Carlos Fortin, Officer-in-Charge of UNCTAD; Mr. Greg Lashutka, Mayor of Columbus; and the representative of Australia.

40. The representative of Australia announced that the City of Melbourne would be prepared to consider hosting a meeting like the Symposium when details of the format became available.

41. The Mayor of Columbus read out a Proclamation of Mayors.

42. Mr. T. A. Manuel (South Africa), Vice-President of the Symposium, declared the Symposium closed.

Annex I

LIST OF DOCUMENTS

TD/SYMP.TE/1	Provisional agenda and annotations for the Senior Officials Segment of the United Nations International Symposium on Trade Efficiency
TD/SYMP.TE/1/Add.1/Rev.1	Provisional agenda and annotations for the Ministerial Segment of the United Nations International Symposium on Trade Efficiency

TD/SYMP.TE/2	Recommendations and guidelines for trade efficiency: Background document prepared by the UNCTAD secretariat
TD/SYMP.TE/3	Compendium of trade facilation recommendations: prepared by the UNCTAD secretariat in cooperation with the ECE Working Party on Facilitation of International Trade Procedures
TD/SYMP.TE/4	Report of the Preparatory Committee for the United Nations International Symposium on Trade Efficiency
TD/SYMP.TE/5	Message received from H. E. Mr. Victor Chernomyrdin, Prime Minister of the Russian Federation
TD/SYMP.TE/6	Report of the United Nations International Symposium on Trade Efficiency
TD/SYMP.TE/7	Summaries of proceedings of the United Nations International Symposium on Trade Efficiency
TD/SYMP.TE/R.1	Draft Columbus Ministerial Declaration on Trade Efficiency
TD/SYMP.TE/R.2	Draft recommendations and guidelines for trade efficiency
TD/SYMP.TE/Misc.1	Provisional list of participants
TD/SYMP.TE/Misc.2/Rev.1	Chairman's summary of the work of the sectoral sessions on policy issues and possible actions for further consideration
TD/SYMP.TE/Misc.3	President's draft summary of issues discussed during the plenary meetings of the Ministerial Meeting
TD/SYMP.TE/INF.1	List of participants

Poland Example

WCO CUSTOMS REFORM AND MODERNIZATION FORUM

"Re-Shaping Customs—a Strategic Outlook"

Brussels, 28–30 April 1997

Customs functions in countries in economic transition

PRESENTATION BY MIECZYSLAW NOGAJ, PRESIDENT OF THE CENTRAL BOARD OF CUSTOMS, REPUBLIC OF POLAND

Distinguished Participants to this Forum, Ladies and Gentlemen,

OPENING REMARKS

I would like to extend my personal thanks and appreciation to Mr. Shaver, Secretary General of the World Customs Organization, and organizers of this very important meeting for this opportunity to speak before you today on the subject of Customs functions in Poland.

The objective of my presentation is to describe the process of reformation and modernization of the Polish Customs administration and to show you its present position. The true starting point of the changes coincided with the years which began the economic transition in Poland—early nineties. Much has been achieved since then but we cannot assume that the work is over. Let me quote an important statement from the theme paper prepared for this meeting ". . . many WCO Members are constantly reviewing strategies and operational methods to bring and keep performance of their public duties in close adjustment to changing business requirements." To meet the challenges which are ahead of us, we cannot allow to slow down the transformation of Customs.

A SHORT INTRODUCTION TO THE DEVELOPMENT
OF ECONOMIC TRANSFORMATION IN POLAND

Following over forty years of a planned economy with foreign trade conducted by a restricted number of specialized enterprises, Poland began a process of radical economic transformation in 1990. Its fundamental rules on foreign trade were laid down in the Law on Economic Activity of 1988 and the Customs Law of 1989 (amended in 1991). The State monopoly and administrative management of foreign trade was abolished and the system was largely liberalized. The Customs tariff became the main trade policy instrument. All economic units acquired the right to carry out foreign trade activities and the number of the companies that the Customs administration had to deal with increased enormously. Today there are well over 100 thousand companies and individual trades in Poland. We witnessed the dramatic growth in quantity and quality of foreign trade turnover and in volume of passenger traffic. These trends were followed by a number of serious threats of rather unknown nature to our Customs only few years ago. To name the most important problems, I should mention smuggling, misdescription of goods, under- or over-valuation, abuse of origin, abuse of temporary admission regimes (including the TIR and ATA carnets), "ghost" businesses and contrived liquidation (companies trading for short periods and going into liquidation to evade payment).

The Polish Customs administration had to face this new economic reality which brought quite new duties and obligations to be fulfilled by Customs officers. Fundamental changes in the way of our Customs work were needed urgently. It was obvious that these changes should lead to facilitation of legitimate trade, that is to ensure that Customs can carry out essential duties, namely the collection of duties, the enforcement of law, both Customs and of other government agencies, and protecting society from illicit drugs, arms, etc., while posing minimum obstacles to that trade. This objective was always remembered in the strategic planning of the Polish Customs administration.

TASKS OF THE CUSTOMS ADMINISTRATION

The basic purpose of the changes in the Customs administration of Poland was to tighten the Customs system and fully integrate it with the Customs systems of Western Europe, as well as to achieve conformity with GATT (later WTO) principles.

This is still valid today at the advanced stage of transformation of our work. To implement such changes the following actions were required:

- necessary changes to Customs law in force, to remove all emerging actual problems and
- adoption and introduction of the new Customs Code and related application rules;
- adaptation of Customs procedures to those used in Western Europe;
- organization of the investigation activity on the legal bases;
- development of the infrastructure (creating new clearance locations, technical equipment and also staff development—by training, recruitment policy, reallocation of human resources, etc.);
- setting up strong co-operation links between our Customs administration and
    —other Customs administrations (to combat more effectively commercial frauds and drug smuggling);
    —international organizations dealing with Customs matters (WCO, DG XXI of EC);
    —Border Guard and Police (to fight against the smuggling of prohibited goods like weapons, drugs, etc.);
    —trade partners (signing Memoranda of Understanding to fight Customs offences);
- computerization of the Customs administration,

to name only the most important of them.

This created the need to undertake both short-term, as well as long-term activities.

• CHANGES IN THE CUSTOMS LAW OF 1989

It soon became apparent that most of the ad hoc changes to the existing Customs Law were not sufficient for the long-term policy of transformation. The Amendments did not remove emerging problems and the need for a new Law was clear to us.

• ADOPTION OF THE NEW CUSTOMS CODE AND RELATED APPLICATION RULES

The project of the new Customs Law was based on a relevant European legal construction—the Community Customs Code. This "new" Law, fully compatible with the European equivalent, had in Polish structure some minor differences concerning mostly terminology, but not procedures.

It was not surprising, I suppose, that we waited for its adoption in the Polish Parliament for a relatively long time. The formal procedure of adoption for this kind of Law is a long and rather painful experience.

The new Polish Customs Code will enter into force this year. All changes comprised in it lead to the introduction of common European standards. The related application rules to the Code will accompany it shortly.

Let me mention at this point that a separate Parliamentary Act dealing with the constitution of our Customs administration is ready and awaiting the legislative procedure.

• ADAPTATION OF CUSTOMS PROCEDURES SIMILAR TO THOSE USED IN WESTERN EUROPE

When Poland started the process of reformation and modernization of its Customs administration, it already was a Contracting Party to the International Convention on the simplification and harmonization of Customs procedures (known as the Kyoto Convention) and accepted ten of the Annexes to this Convention. Five more of them were accepted in 1994 but among them there were not the most important Annexes:

Annex B.1. concerning clearance for home use and Annex C.1. concerning outright exportation. The reason for the exclusion of these Annexes from the acceptance was the structure of the Customs Law of 1989 and the necessity of entering a lot of reservations to them.

With the new Customs Code we will be much more opened to the simplification and harmonization of Customs procedures. I am glad to add that we fully support the revision of the Kyoto Convention which is at the moment one of the top priorities of the World Customs Organization and we believe that it will play a vital role in modernization work of the Customs administration in Poland.

There are naturally many other international Conventions which are essential to any modem Customs administration. They were taken into account in our process of reformation and we are now a Contracting Party to most of them. Let me just mention at the moment

—the International Convention on the Harmonized Commodity Description and Coding System;

  (Poland uses Combined Nomenclature of the European Union at 8 digit level, which is compatible with EU CN. Polish CN is continuously adjusted to EU CN);

—the Convention on Temporary Admission (the Istanbul Convention);

  (evaluation of the above mentioned Convention is in progress; it will be decided which Annexes to this Convention should be accepted in the near future);

—Article VII of the WTO Agreement (Customs Value Code);

    (adopted in the Polish Customs Code; Poland introduced a new form for the Declaration of Customs Value—based on European D.V. 1 and D.V. 1 BIS);

—the SAD Convention and the Common Transit Convention;

    (the Polish Customs administration changed its national rules and since 1996 has become a Contracting Party to the above mentioned Conventions; all forms required for transit are completed in accordance with the Transit Convention, the others—according to the SAD Convention and the national regulations).

This approach allowed us to adopt Customs procedures which are commonly used in Western Europe.

ORGANIZATION OF THE INVESTIGATION ACTIVITY ON THE LEGAL BASES

Investigation activity is a crucial part of any modern Customs administration. This activity had to be organized practically from scratch. The process was rather slow at the beginning because of lack of human and financial recourses. I should like to stress here that it was the PHARE programme that at that difficult time provided the Polish Customs administration with a substantial amount of high technology equipment (anti-smuggling, anti-drug and other detection equipment, including chemical anti-drug tests and short-range communication equipment). PHARE also provided relevant training sessions for the officers of our administration and the support of highly qualified EU specialists.

It took us some time to find proper legal basis for this kind of activity.

While raising the issue of Customs investigation I am glad to note the development of the Eastern and Central Europe RILO situated in Warsaw which gives support and assistance to Investigation Services in the region. I am satisfied that the RILO-WARSAW is accepted by many Customs enforcement bodies co-operating with it. Having in mind the fact that RILO network is a very important source of information to any Customs Investigation Services, we created last year the National Customs Intelligence Unit. This should improve the flow of information and its use in our investigation area.

DEVELOPMENT OF THE INFRASTRUCTURE —BORDER CROSSING DIFFICULTIES —STAFF DEVELOPMENT

Border Crossing Difficulties

You might be surprised to hear that the average time of Customs clearance of a single truck on Polish border crossing points is not longer than 2.5 minutes. We also hear that the average waiting time of trucks at the border may be measured in days in some cases. I would like to clarify this fact. The main reason for border delays of traffic is not the slow action of the Customs officers but the infrastructure constraints rather.

The infrastructure is insufficient and outdated but at present it is being rebuilt. We observe that the volume of traffic is rising systematically, while the capacity of the road border crossing points remains mostly on the same level. The Polish Customs administration supports modernization but for the time being the road border crossings are the responsibility of Local Government and the road network is the responsibility of the Directorate of Public Roads. Modernization of the road border crossing points is in progress but this kind of work usually takes years to see results.

Staff Development

It was obvious at all stages of our current changes that the effectiveness of the Customs administration could be guaranteed by changes in the system of recruitment, promotion and training of Customs officers. In early nineties there were 3.5 thousand of them, today there are over 13 thousand. The creation of a modern and effective training system was one of the principle tasks.

Today the training organization acting within our administration is very strong. The training function has been designated to the Training Office which is responsible for policy, assessment of training needs, design and methodologies, strategy and planning. There are two residential training centres in Poland and they are very well equipped. Training covers new areas, e.g. a new programme of management development for future management staff.

We are doing our best to improve social conditions of the employees, enhance their qualifications and promote officers who have university education. It is obvious that financial motivation plays a very important role, especially in the case of recruitment of university graduates. The new proposals are under consideration in the Ministry of Finance. I hope that we will find solutions improving the work conditions of our Customs officers.

SETTING UP STRONG CO-OPERATION LINKS BETWEEN THE POLISH CUSTOMS ADMINISTRATION AND —OTHER CUSTOMS ADMINISTRATIONS, —INTERNATIONAL ORGANIZATIONS, —BORDER GUARD AND POLICE, —TRADE PARTNERS

It might be interesting to note that in many cases it was necessary to establish or renew many international links from the very beginning. Due to political changes in Eastern Europe, in the early nineties Poland found itself in the neighbourhood of entirely new states. Some of them had to create their state administration, including the Customs, from the starting point.

Poland has concluded 19 bilateral Agreements regarding mutual assistance in Customs matters (this number includes the Agreements with all neighbouring Customs administrations). Assistance allowed within the framework of these Agreements helps us to ensure that Customs law is properly observed and to prevent, investigate and combat offences against Customs legislation.

The importance of co-operation with other Customs administrations, agencies and trade partners was stressed on frequent occasions by the World Customs Organization. Many programmes initiated by this international organization were implemented by our Customs. They were, and are at the moment, the integral part of the modernization process of our administration.

Computerization

It is often stated that automation of the Customs is the element which can solve many problems. That is true, but some strategic points of modernization mentioned earlier in this presentation condition the computerization process. The most important of them are: firm Customs law and regulations, simplified and harmonized Customs procedures, trained staff ready to use computerized system.

Automation process of the Polish Customs administration is quite advanced. The PHARE Programme Management Unit in the Central Board of Customs is implementing the POLCUSTOMS Project which will provide the Customs with the E-mail and several computer systems creating together the Central Management System.

Again I would like to stress how important the PHARE assistance is for successful completion of our project and the computerization as a whole.

CLOSING REMARKS

Distinguished Participants to this Forum, Ladies and Gentlemen,

The role of the Customs in Poland is now not much different from the role of the Customs administrations all over the world and especially in the countries of Western Europe.

Its main tasks are:

—the facilitation of legitimate trade,

—the collection of revenue to the State budget,

—the enforcement of law and protection of society from drugs, arms, etc.

The specific character of our situation is that it is expected from the Polish Customs to fulfill its general task and meet a number of additional challenges simultaneously.

The time allowed for our adaptation to the Customs Systems of Western Europe is relatively short while "more and more international consignments are passing over national frontiers within integrated global supply, production arid distribution networks, supported by reliable delivery services", as it has been stated in the opening paragraph of the theme paper to this Forum.

Let me assure you that the Polish Customs administration will make every effort to meet the challenges created by the rapid development of trade in Poland and will not pose obstacles to that trade.

For many Customs administrations it is not easy to operate smoothly in the fast changing environment conditioned by many factors of economic, political and social nature. I have to stress that in our case we are successful. This is due to the proper definition of tasks and the consequence in fulfilling these objectives.

I am sure that the Forum will find the answer to the important problem how Customs, business and inter-institutional consultation and co~operation, could be stimulated and motivated to meet the needs of many WCO Members asking for assistance.

Thank you for your kind attention.

IMF Integrity Paper

INTERNATIONAL MONETARY FUND
FISCAL AFFAIRS DEPARTMENT

Practical Measures to Promote Integrity
in Customs Administrations

John Crotty
Chief Tax Administration Division

PRACTICAL MEASURES TO PROMOTE INTEGRITY IN CUSTOMS ADMINISTRATIONS

The purpose of this paper is to outline an approach to promoting integrity (reducing corruption) in customs administrations. While it outlines some of the general factors that lead to corruption, the paper does not deal at length with the reasons for or causes of corruption nor the economic impact of such practices. It accepts, as a given, that opportunities exist in all revenue-collecting agencies to engage in corrupt practices. Based on this reality, it attempts to provide the framework for the legal and administrative procedures that are necessary to detect, punish, and reduce such undesirable behavior.

The paper draws upon the experiences of the Tax Administration Division of the Fiscal Affairs Department. In this respect it reflects not only the technical assistance advice provided to various countries but also the experiences of staff of the division in dealing with issues of corruption in the management of revenue departments in their own countries.[1] Its central theme is that there is no easy or quick solution to the issue of integrity in customs administrations (e.g., higher salaries or computerization) but that a comprehensive approach is necessary to put the required measures in place and to ensure that they operate effectively over time. Following a brief summary of the principal causes of corruption, the paper sets out the main elements of a plan to promote integrity in customs administration, namely: a clear, well understood policy framework; simple, transparent procedures; a professional customs administration; performance standards; a code of conduct; effective internal audit; and administrative autonomy. In support of these elements, there should also be an atmosphere that encourages members of the trade community to come forward and discuss their issues with the administration, an independent honest judicial system, and a press that is interested, able, and allowed to raise issues of corruption.

Causes of corruption

In reviewing the causes of corruption, it is important to address not only the overall factors which may lead to corrupt practices but also the specific nature and causes of corruption in customs administrations. General factors include: extensive intervention of the Government in the economy; cultural norms and practices that influence the behavior of administrators; centralized decision making; excessive discretionary power in the hands of administrators; lack of supervision and guidance; lack of accountability; and inadequate control systems. In addition to these general factors, it must be recognised that incentives and opportunities to engage in corrupt practices are likely to arise in revenue administrations than in many other areas of government administration. Nobody likes to pay taxes. Therefore, the taxpayer will take every opportunity and make every effort to reduce the tax burden. This may include the bribing of a revenue official, especially if there is a high probability that the official will accept the bribe and a concomitant minimal risk to both parties that the receipt of the bribe will be detected or sanctioned. In the case of customs transactions, the incentive goes beyond just the desire to reduce the tax burden, as the importer is also interested in obtaining the goods as fast as possible and may take the opportunity to "facilitate" their release.

The most important factors that lead to lack of integrity in the administration of duties and taxes include:

- *complex and restrictive tax and foreign trade systems that lead to rent seeking and corrupt behavior*—The rules may be so complex that importers and exporters have no choice but to meet face-to-face with an official to seek an explanation or the exercise of the discretionary power that the official may possess. This is often compounded by the lack of information that allows importers and exporters to determine their liability and comply voluntarily with the law.

- *high tax and tariff rates*—The higher the tax rates, the greater the incentive to engage in corrupt practices to reduce this burden. A dramatic example of this is in the area of high excises, particularly on tobacco and alcohol, where organized crime is involved in the bribery of revenue officials, resulting in widespread illegal production and smuggling of these goods.

- *exemptions*—In addition to exemptions that are provided for in the law, discretionary exemptions that can be granted by the Ministers and/or the head of the customs administration, create the opportunity to engage in corrupt practices. They undermine the fairness of the system and may create, in the mind of the importers who are paying the duties and taxes, a doubt about the reasonableness of continuing to comply.

- *complex and bureaucratic procedures*—Instead of making it easy for importers and exporters to voluntarily comply and pay the taxes, multiple forms and steps are often introduced that require stops at many desks and visits to many offices each one associated with a "fee" to facilitate processing.

- *weak control systems*—Too little attention is paid to the implementation of systems that make it difficult for officials to engage in corrupt practices. Individuals take into account the perceived threat of being detected when they decide to engage in corrupt practices and, if the risk is low, many more will be willing to take the risk.

- *lack of effective disciplinary measures*—Sanctions are an important factor in deterring corrupt behavior. If the penalties are not severe enough and applied each time that inappropriate behavior is detected, they will not be effective in reducing corruption.

- *lack of professionalism*—Too often employment in customs administrations is seen as an opportunity to work for a short period of time to enrich oneself and not as a long-term professional career.

Building a system to promote integrity

Building a system to promote integrity in customs administration requires not only the effort to put in place the necessary measures to combat corruption but also on-going vigilance to ensure that the measures continue to operate as intended. Even in those countries that are considered to have the most efficient and honest administrations, considerable effort is still invested to ensure that the controls continue to operate and that corrupt behavior is detected and dealt with. Threats are always present. For example, in countries with generally low tax and tariff rates, criminals involved in drug smuggling have the ability to pay large amounts of money to a customs officer to allow a shipment of drugs to proceed without inspection.

In order to deal effectively with corruption, at the outset, there must be a clear and unequivocal commitment from the Government to address the problem. This goes beyond mere statements that corruption will not be tolerated

---

IT CAN'T HAPPEN HERE

In one country that has a reputation for integrity in its public service, in general, and the customs administration, in particular, recent cases of collusion with organized crime have been detected related to the smuggling of goods with high excises. When this was discovered, there was, on the one hand, shock that such practices had taken place and, on the other hand, satisfaction that the systems were in place to discover the corrupt behavior.

---

to the actual actions of Ministers and other high ranking government officials. In some countries, senior officials believe and act as if they are above the law and demand special treatment from customs officials (e.g., proceeding through customs without paying duty and taxes on high value purchases acquired abroad). When this sort of thing happens, a powerful example is set by senior officials which others will surely follow. Once the commitment has been made to address corruption problems, senior officials must take the responsibility to lead the customs administration by the example of their own strict compliance with the laws. There are also other essential steps that should be taken to build a system based on integrity that will produce the revenue returns expected by the Government. They are discussed below.

1. Clear, well understood policy framework

Simplification of the tax system (e.g., reducing the number of rates to the minimum and restricting exemptions) is not only good economic policy but it also reduces the opportunities for corruption. From a customs administrator's point of view, simple, clear legislation creates the framework for the development of systems and procedures that are easily understood by both the trade community and the officials. This policy framework should be based on the following principles:

- *minimum number of rates*—Rationalization of tax and tariff rates and clear definitions of how and when different rates apply reduce the need for interpretation by administrators and the face-to-face negotiations that may result in the exchange of money for a favorable ruling.
- *low rates*—If it is generally perceived that the system is fair and that the rates of tax are reasonable, there is less incentive to become involved in fraudulent activities.
- *minimum exemptions*—While it is virtually impossible to eliminate all exemptions, tax legislation should be written to clearly specify exemptions in the law and to eliminate the discretionary power of Ministers or government officials to grant exemptions.
- *minimum nontariff barriers to foreign trade*—The need for numerous approvals for foreign trade licenses and multi-agency authorization to import and export, creates the opportunity and incentive to engage in corrupt practices.

ONE ADMINISTRATOR'S EXPERIENCE

In response to a question concerning the impact of the newly implemented VAT on customs administration, the head of one local office in an eastern European country responded: "The tax is easy to administer because there is only one rate and the exemptions are provided for in the law. There is no room for negotiation."

- *effective penalty system*—A good penalty system should provide the administrator with the ability to impose administrative penalties for minor offences. This may include fines, for example, for broken seals on vehicles transporting goods in-transit and presentation of declarations with an unacceptable level of errors. Serious cases of fraud, including the bribing of revenue officials, should result in more serious actions, including criminal prosecution.

- *provide an independent appeal mechanism*—Every tax law, no matter how well written, is capable of being interpreted differently. In order to preserve the independence of the officials and the integrity of the system, it is important that taxpayers have the ability to challenge decisions and can be assured of a fair hearing both in the customs administration and by the courts. Court decisions should be widely publicized by the customs administration and in the press.

In addition to a clear and simple policy framework, there is also a need to separate the setting of policy from its administration. The policy makers should ensure that their objectives are met during the policy development process and the drafting of legislation, including holding appropriate discussions with the trade community to ascertain their views. However, once the policy has been established and provided for in the law, extra-statutory concessions should not be used by the policy makers to facilitate more favorable treatment for influential importers and exporters. It should not be the responsibility of senior policy makers or Ministers to review and rule on individual cases. By way of example, it might be noted that the customs administrations in the United States and the United Kingdom, have clearly established rules supporting this separation of responsibilities.

2. Simple, transparent procedures

It is the responsibility of the customs administrators to put in place simple, easily understood systems and procedures. The reasons for this approach are twofold. Firstly, it reduces the compliance costs for the importers and exporters and, secondly, it reduces the opportunities for corruption.

The most important principle in the design of simple, straight forward customs procedures is self-declaration. Importers should have the capability to determine their duty and tax liabilities and, based on their understanding of the law, to present to the customs administration a declaration that includes a calculation of the amounts owing. This must be supported by documentation and information as requested by the administration and is, of course, subject to verification, either at time of presentation or later through post-release review. To be fully effective and thereby reduce the opportunities for corruption, the self-declaration system should be based on the following:

- *one step process*—A customs declaration should be lodged at the reception counter of the customs office and the paperwork processed by the administration with no further need for contact, until that processing has been completed.

- *minimize the information and documentation requirements*—Customs administrations must define their information and documentation needs in a way that minimizes administrative requirements upon the importers and exporters. For example, the customs declaration can be used for multiple purposes (e.g., calculation and payment of duties and taxes and preparation of foreign trade statistics).

- *consistent interpretations*—Importers can only be expected to self-declare their liabilities in an environment where the interpretation of the laws is consistent and procedures are standardized, with each transaction treated in the same way as the previous one.

- *computerization*—The introduction of computerized support for the processing of customs documents, perhaps more than any other change, provides the opportunity to implement standardized procedures that leave little to the discretion of the officials. A properly designed system ensures that the correct rates of duties and taxes are applied; exemptions are only granted to authorized organizations and for authorized goods and services; the required information and documentation is presented; timeframes for payment are met; and those who do not comply with filing and payment timeframes are identified and follow-up action is taken. In addition, the system can provide useful management information including, for example, identifying transactions that do not meet time standards for processing or individual officers who undertake actions that are out of the ordinary (e.g., physically inspecting too many shipments).

3. Professional customs administrations

The development of professional customs administrations is important, not only to improve the effectiveness of these administrations, but at the same time, to address issues of corruption. Too often, governments are unwilling to

---

UNEXPECTED BENEFIT

In one country, foreign experts were hired to work with the local customs administration, to set up and operate anti-smuggling teams. Not only has large scale smuggling been detected but, in addition, specific cases of corrupt officers and offices have also been identified.

provide the authority to the administrations to enforce the laws or to invest the resources necessary to build and provide ongoing support for efficient and effective administration. Experience in developed countries has shown that the best way to ensure fairness and neutrality in the administration of the tax system is to develop professional administrations with clearly defined responsibilities and accountability for performance, including:

- *professional management*—It is important that the customs administrations include skilled, knowledgeable supervisors and managers. Too often senior officials in the administrations change as governments change and individuals with little or no knowledge of legislation, regulations, systems, and procedures are put in charge of revenue collection and trade facilitation. In these circumstances, staff may perceive that they have limited career opportunities in the organization, little, if any, "loyalty" to the organization and, perhaps, may be more open to corruption. For those who join a customs organization for the term of a new government, working in that organization may be seen as a reward and an opportunity to enrich themselves, through the provision of exemptions and other concessions to the business community.

  Management controls are an essential component of well-run customs administrations. This includes: a clear statement of goals and objectives; well documented operating procedures; supervision of day-to-day activities; and a regular review of the outputs of employees. Management will also consider the results of its internal audit processes, feedback from importers and exporters, and the views of its employees in evaluating its operations.

- *compensation and working conditions*—Customs administrators must be provided with sufficient compensation to reduce the incentive to engage in corrupt practices. While civil service pay can never be at a level that will eliminate all corrupt behavior (e.g., there are many reported cases of well paid customs officers in developed countries who have accepted tens of thousands of dollars to allow a shipment of drugs to pass through the border), compensation can be set at a level that provides a good standard of living and eliminates the need to accept "facilitation fees". In recognition that it may not be possible to address low civil service pay in general, some countries have implemented special pay scales and incentives for staff in revenue agencies.

  The provision of appropriate working conditions is also important. This includes proper office space, equipment (e.g., telephones, computers, and transportation), and supplies.

  The administration should not have to rely on importers, exporters, or their agents to provide any facilities or equipment which could imply that a favor is expected in return.

STAFF ROTATION

It is a standard procedure in customs administrations in developed countries to assign officers to process passengers and cargo at certain work locations and to provide the work rotation schedule, only after the officer has reported for work.

- *staff rotation*—Any regulatory agency is better able to carry out its functions in an impartial manner if it remains at arms length from those it is charged with regulating. Revenue agencies are no different in this regard. Accordingly, it is important that staff rotations take place on a regular basis to reduce opportunities for collusion with those importers and exporters with whom customs officers may be in regular contact.

- *training*—Staff training is crucial to the development of professional customs administrations. It is particularly important that a careful analysis of the training needs of the organization and its staff is completed to ensure that the training that is delivered matches their needs of the staff. (This is a difficult enough task for the most modern customs administrations.) Too often, new legislation and procedures are introduced with inadequate attention given to staff training needs. In addition to improving technical skills, training can also serve to build "esprit de corps" and to emphasize responsibility and loyalty to the organization, thereby promoting integrity.

- *merit-based promotions*—An important component in establishing a professional administration is to provide a clearly defined career path and promotion policy that is clearly based on merit. Each employee must feel that there is an opportunity to advance, based on hard work, and that to engage in inappropriate behavior will jeopardize this opportunity (and lead to dismissal in serious cases).

- *recruitment*—As part of the plan to develop professional administrations, it is important that the personnel requirements be clearly defined, including the educational and other requirements of those being hired. Revenue administrations, because of restrictive civil service rules, are often unable to hire people with the necessary background and skills required to carry out specialist tasks.

- *separation of responsibilities*—The creation of a functional organization is one of the most effective ways of combating corruption. Too often, individual officers are assigned the responsibility for all activities related to an importer or exporter. This invites collusion and the granting of favors. Through the separation of responsibilities, checks and balances are built into the system. For example, the processing of a customs declaration and physical inspection of goods, when carried out by different officers, can reduce the opportunity to influence decisions, for example, related to the classification and valuation of goods.

- *complaint monitoring*—Administrations should establish a special unit for the receipt of complaints concerning the performance of officials.

4. Performance standards[2]

Building on a base that includes transparent legislation, streamlined procedures, customs administrations should put in place performance standards that enable policy makers, management, and the public to measure how well an administration is performing. This has several advantages. Firstly, it enables the policy makers including Ministers to hold heads of administrations accountable, if agreed standards are not met. Secondly, it enables management to measure the performance of offices and individuals and to identify potential problems. Thirdly, it makes very clear to the employees that their performance will be measured against clearly defined standards. Fourthly, the public is aware of what is expected and, therefore, should be willing and encouraged to bring to the attention of management any cases where the standards have not been met.

Too often, the only performance standard established for the administrations is the requirement to meet certain revenue targets. This is not enough, particularly if corruption is a problem. A corrupt revenue administration may, over the short term, be able to meet revenue targets. However, achieving such a target may have little to do with a consistent application of the law to all taxpayers and more to do with its overzealous application to a more limited number of those taxpayers. Performance standards, in revenue administrations, should include the following:

- *revenue targets*—Customs administrations should participate in discussions leading to the setting of revenue targets. The administrators should also be invited to provide an assessment of the practicability of policy proposals being considered by Government, and the feasibility of collecting projected revenues. Once overall targets for a customs administration have been agreed, it is the responsibility of the administration to establish the targets for each of its offices and to put in place the mechanism for monitoring performance against these targets.

- *service standards*—In customs administrations, there should be clearly articulated standards for the various functions that are performed. For importers, it is very important that they know the time that the goods will be under customs control, as this can significantly impact estimates of inventory requirements. By establishing service standards and making them known to staff and to importers and exporters, an administration can establish monitoring mechanisms to identify transactions, offices, and officers that do not meet the required standards. Reports from the monitoring system may also help to identify areas that should be investigated for potential corrupt practices.

- *post-release review*—an effective post-release review program[3] should include performance standards that assist in the monitoring of these activities.

5. Code of conduct

It is important that employees and importers and exporters be aware of the conduct that is expected of all parties. By clearly articulating expectations, customs administrations can hold employees accountable for poor performance and take appropriate action when these standards are not met. Many administrations publish a "code of conduct" setting out these expectations. For such a code to be effective, it must also include a description of the disciplinary actions that will be taken if unacceptable behavior is discovered (to be effective, disciplinary actions must be taken on a consistent basis). It must also be recognised that the political and social context of a particular country significantly determine the rules of acceptable conduct of officials and that the rules guiding their participation in activities outside their official responsibilities can vary from country to country. However, the code would normally include the following:

- *maintaining integrity*—The acceptance of gifts, favors, or benefits that may influence decisions is not permitted. Disciplinary action up to and including dismissal is normally taken in cases where employees accept a gift of any significant value.

- *confidentiality of information*—Information from customs declarations as well as that obtained from post-release reviews is confidential and, as such, must not be disclosed in an unauthorized manner.

- *conflict of interest*—Employees would normally be prohibited from engaging in activities that are in clear conflict with their official position. For example, a customs officer would not be permitted to own a customs brokerage business or to engage in any business that involves extensive import and export activities. Many administrations also have a requirement that employees disclose their assets at time of hiring, and update this information on a regular basis so that their managers can detect, at an early stage, if an employee has accrued assets that are inconsistent with the level of compensation received by the employee.

- *appearance and conduct*—Standards for appearance and conduct normally include: observing the hours of duty; dressing appropriately; dealing courteously with the taxpaying public; prohibiting the use of intoxicants in the work place; and using government equipment, including vehicles, only for business purposes.

6. Effective internal audit

While it is the overall responsibility of management to monitor performance and to ensure that operational policies are being followed and performance standards are being met, this must be supplemented by effective internal audit. Usually, the internal audit department reports to the head of the administration and is responsible for carrying out regular reviews of all operations in the organization. It is often the internal auditors in customs administrations who are the first to detect instances of corruption when reviewing compliance with procedures.[4] Serious cases of corruption, involving violations of the law, are usually turned over to law enforcement officials for criminal prosecution. Internal audit activities normally include the following:

- *compliance with operational procedures*—Based on clearly defined procedures which would normally be laid out in manuals or procedure guides, an auditor reviews the actual operation of the customs offices. This would include, for example, reviews of declaration processing and procedures for the selection of shipments for physical inspection.

- *expenditure/use of government funds/assets*—There are opportunities in the administration of large government departments to mis-appropriate funds and it is one of the roles of internal audit to review activities related, for example, to the purchasing of supplies, awarding of contracts, and hiring personnel (e.g., some countries have a serious problem with "ghost workers" on the payroll).

7. Administrative autonomy

In recent years, one strategy that has been followed by a number of countries for improving the effectiveness of customs administration and to address, among other issues, corruption, has been to increase the autonomy of the administration. While there are a number of alternatives to providing greater autonomy, most share the following common features: a degree of financial independence, in the sense that the administrations are able to allocate budget funds as they consider appropriate; administrative independence, meaning that the administrations are provided the authority to formulate their own administrative policies and objectives; and independence from general civil service personnel requirements, meaning that the administrations are responsible for their own recruitment, salary structure, career path and training, and establishing performance standards and a code of conduct.

Given appropriate checks and balances on such customs administrations and a willingness on the part of Government not to interfere in day-to-day operations, increased autonomy may facilitate the implementation of measures to increase integrity and combat corruption.

Other important considerations

There are also other important considerations that can affect the ability of a customs administration to build an organization based on integrity and to effectively address corruption issues. While these may relate more to the political and social framework and the history of a country they can still greatly affect efforts to implement measures of the kind outlined in this paper.

- *Is it possible to create an atmosphere where importers and exporters will come forward and discuss the decisions that are being made?*—The seeking of information and entering into a reasonable dialogue concerning the interpretation of the legislation and procedures are important features of a good customs system. Too often, however, this tradition does not exist in a country and can be very difficult to foster. Foreign-owned companies may be familiar with this practice in their home countries but may be reluctant to enter into discussions on issues of interpretation of the law in a country where corruption is widespread, for fear that they may be asked for a bribe (which, under the laws in their home country, they are required to report). They may often prefer to pay a fee to a middle man to intercede on their behalf and not request a detailed explanation of how the fee is used. In some countries where decision-making continues to be highly centralized in the bureaucracy, there may also be a serious reluctance to seek review of decisions on customs issues because of the inordinate amount of time that may be required to obtain a ruling.

- *Does an independent judiciary exist?*—Important customs related issues will end up in court, if the issues cannot be settled through the review processes in a customs administration. Even if a professional customs administration is established, the work of that organization to ensure a high level of compliance with the revenue laws can lose much of its impact if a corrupt judicial system undermines its effectiveness. For example, corrupt members of the judiciary may overturn sound decisions taken related to interpretations of customs legislation, criminal prosecutions for fraud, and prosecutions of corrupt employees.

- *Is there freedom of the press?*—It is often the press that exposes cases of corruption in Government. They have an important role to play in reporting on official decisions (for example, the granting of exemptions) and in exposing instances of corruption by officials.

Absent a broader political and social framework that provides strong support for measures to address corruption problems in a customs service (including an independent judiciary and a free press), it may be very difficult to sustain efforts to establish a high integrity customs administration. But that is not to say that changes of the kind discussed in this paper should not be implemented. It is merely to acknowledge that their impact may not be so far reaching in the longer term.

NOTES

1. This paper draws extensively on two previous papers of the staff of the Tax Administration Division: "Integrity in Customs: Action Program for Policy Makers and Customs Administrators", A. Goorman, presented to the Customs Cooperation Council (CCC), 1993 and "Corruption in Tax Administration", P. Dos Santos, presented to the Inter-American Center of Tax Administrators (CIAT) 1995.

2. For more detailed discussions on issues related to performance standards, see a paper titled "Performance Standards in Tax Administration" presented by John Crotty at the 1996 annual meeting of the CIAT.

3. Post-release reviews are undertaken after goods have been released from Customs control by specialist officers who typically review valuation, tariff classification, origin, and any other conditions that determine the duties and taxes payable.

4. In some administrations, there is also a separate organization (e.g., an Internal Affairs department) that is specifically responsible for detecting and dealing with cases of corruption, including the misappropriation of funds. If management or internal audit uncovers any cases of corruption, they are automatically turned over to this organization.

Arusha Declaration

DECLARATION OF THE CUSTOMS CO-OPERATION COUNCIL CONCERNING INTEGRITY IN CUSTOMS

The Customs Co-operation Council

NOTING that Customs is an essential instrument for the effective management of an economy and that it performs simultaneously the vital roles of combating smuggling and facilitating the flow of legitimate trade.

ACKNOWLEDGING that:

- corruption can destroy the efficient functioning of any society and diminish the ability of the Customs to accomplish its mission;
- a corrupt Customs
    - —will not deliver the revenue that is properly due to the State,
    - —will not be effective in the fight against illicit trafficking, and
    - —will obstruct the growth of legitimate international trade and hinder economic development;
- the Customs has no right to public recognition or trust if its staff break the law habitually.

CONSIDERING that corruption can be combated effectively only as part of a comprehensive national effort;

DECLARES that a top priority for all Governments should be to ensure that Customs is free of corruption. This requires a firm commitment at the highest political and administrative levels to maintaining a high standard of integrity throughout the civil service and particularly in the Customs.

DECLARES that a national Customs integrity programme must take account of the following key factors:

1. Customs legislation should be clear and precise. Import tariffs should be moderated where possible. The number of rates should be limited. Administrative regulation of trade should be reduced to the absolute minimum. There should be as few exemptions to the standard rules as possible.

2. Customs procedures should be simple, consistent, and easily accessible, and should include a procedure for appealing against decisions of the Customs, with the possibility of recourse to independent adjudication in the final instance. They could be based on the Kyoto Convention and should be so framed as to reduce to a minimum the inappropriate exercise of discretion.

3. Automation (including EDI) is a powerful tool against corruption, and its utilization should have priority.

4. In order to reduce the opportunities for malpractice, Customs managers should employ such measures as strategic segregation of functions, rotation of assignments and random allocation of examinations among Customs officers and, in certain circumstances, regular relocation of staff.

5. Line managers should have prime responsibility for identifying weaknesses in working methods and in the integrity of their staff, and for taking steps to rectify such weaknesses.

6. Internal and external auditing are essential, effective internal auditing being a particularly useful means of ensuring that Customs procedures are appropriate and are being implemented correctly. The internal auditing arrangements should be complemented by an internal affairs unit that has the specific task of investigating all cases of suspected malpractice.

7. The management should instil in its officers loyalty and pride in their service, an "esprit de corps" and a desire to cooperate in measures to reduce their exposure to the possibility of corruption.

8. The processes for the recruitment and advancement of Customs officers should be objective and immune from interference. They should include a means of identifying applicants who have, and are likely to maintain, a high standard of personal ethics.

9. Customs officers should be issued with a Code of Conduct, the implications of which should be fully explained to them. There should be effective disciplinary measures, which should include the possibility of dismissal.

10. Customs officers should receive adequate professional training throughout their careers, which should include coverage of ethics and integrity issues.

11. The remuneration received by Customs officers should be sufficient to afford them a decent standard of living, and may in certain circumstances include social benefits such as health care and housing facilities, and/or incentive payments (bonuses, rewards, etc.).

12. Customs administrations should foster an open and transparent relationship with Customs brokers and with the relevant sectors of the business community. Liaison committees are useful in this respect.

Made at Arusha, Tanzania on the 7th day of July, 1993 (81st/82nd Council Sessions)

Code of Conduct

U.S. CUSTOMS SERVICE
SUMMARY OF THE CODE OF CONDUCT
AND
STANDARD OF ETHICAL CONDUCT

As employees of the U.S. Customs Service, we are bound by the general rules of ethics and conduct that apply to all Federal employees. In addition, there are rules of conduct contained in Customs' own code of conduct that supplements the Federal policy. Specifically, we are guided by:

1. Executive Order 12731, October 17,1990, <u>Prescribing Standards of Ethical Conduct for all Executive Branch employees.</u>
2. 5 CFR 2635, <u>Standards of Ethical Conduct for Employees of the Executive Branch</u> (Office of Government Ethics), and 5 CFR 3101, <u>Supplemental Standards of Ethical Conduct for Employees of the Department of the Treasury.</u>
3. U.S. Customs Service "Policy and Procedure Manual", Chapter 51735, <u>Conduct and Employee Responsibilities.</u>

The following is a **_SUMMARY_** of some of the applicable rules governing conduct of Customs employees. For more specific, detailed guidance, refer to the specific directive or policy.

SUMMARY OF 5 CFR 2635

GENERAL PROVISIONS:

5 CFR 2635 establishes as a government employee there are some basic obligations of public service and general principles which apply to every employee. These general principles are:

1. Public service is a public trust, requiring employees to place loyalty to the Constitution, the laws and ethical principles above private gain.

2. Employees shall not hold financial interests that conflict with the conscientious performance of duty.

3. Employees shall not engage in financial transactions using nonpublic Government information or allow the improper use of such information to further any private interest.

4. An employee shall not, without certain approved exceptions, solicit or accept any gift or other item of monetary value from any person or entity seeking official action from, doing business with, or conducting activities regulated by the U.S. Customs Service, or whose interests may be substantially affected by the performance or nonperformance of the employee's duties.

5. Employees shall put forth honest effort in the performance of their duties.

6. Employees shall not knowingly make unauthorized commitments or promises of any kind purporting to bind the Government.

7. Employees shall not use public office for private gain.

8. Employees shall act impartially and not give preferential treatment to any private organization or individual.

9. Employees shall protect and conserve Federal property and shall not use it for other than authorized activities.

10. Employees shall not engage in outside employment or activities, including seeking or negotiating for employment, that conflict with official Government duties and responsibilities.

11. Employees shall disclose waste, fraud, abuse, and corruption to appropriate authorities.

12. Employees shall satisfy in good faith their obligations as citizens, including all just financial obligations, especially those such as Federal, State, or local taxes that are imposed by law.

13. Employees shall adhere to all laws and regulations that provide equal opportunity for all Americans regardless of race, color, religion, sex, national origin, age, or handicap.

14. Employees shall endeavor to avoid any actions creating the appearance that they are violating the law or the ethical standards set forth in this part. Whether particular circumstances create an appearance that the law or these standards have been violated shall be determined from the perspective of a reasonable person with knowledge of the relevant facts.

ETHICS ADVICE

As required by 5 CFR 2635, each agency must designate an ethics official who is responsible for coordinating and managing the agency's ethics program, which is the Office of Chief Counsel for the Customs Service. The designated agency ethics official (DAEO) is responsible for providing ethics counseling and advice regarding ethics issues.

Employees having questions regarding the applications of ethics rules shall direct them to the DAEO or the appropriate Associate or Assistant Chief Counsel. Questions should be in writing and contain all relevant facts. Obtaining advice from the DAEO, particularly in writing, helps protect the employee by acting on "good faith" advice received.

GIFTS

5 CFR 2635 contains standards that prohibit an employee from soliciting or accepting any gift from a prohibited source or given because of the employee's official position unless the item is excluded from the definition of a gift or falls within one of the exceptions.

As a general rule, an employee shall not directly or indirectly:

1. Solicit coerce or accept a gift from a <u>prohibited source</u>; or
2. accept a gift given because of the employee's official position; or
3. accept a gift in return for being influenced in the performance of an official act; or
4. accept gifts from the same or different sources on a basis so frequent that a reasonable person would be led to believe the employee is using his public office for private gain; or
5. Accept a gift in violation of any statute. Generally, this is referring to bribery statutes, i.e., accepting a gift or payment for failing to perform official duties properly.

A gift is defined as any gratuity, favor, discount, entertainment, hospitality, loan, forbearance, or other item having monetary value. It includes services as well as gifts of training, transportation, local travel, lodgings and meals, whether provided in-kind, by purchase or a ticket, payment in advance or reimbursement after the expense has been incurred. It does not include:

1. Modest items of food and refreshments;
2. Greeting cards and items with little intrinsic value, such as plaques, and trophies;
3. Certain loans from banks and other financial institutions;
4. Certain commercial discounts;
5. Rewards and prizes given to competitors in contests or events open to the public;
6. Pension and other benefits resulting from previous employment;
7. Anything which is paid for by the Government or secured by the Government under Government contract;

8. Any gift accepted by the Government under specific statutory authority; or

9. Anything for which market value is paid by the employee.

A prohibited source means any person who:

1. Is seeking official action by the Customs Service;

2. Does business or seeks to do business with the Customs Service;

3. Conducts activities regulated by the Customs Service;

4. Has interests that may be substantially affected by employee's performance; or

5. Is an organization a majority of whose members are described above.

Exceptions to Acceptance of Gift Prohibitions:

The prohibitions against acceptance of a gift identified above do not apply if the gift is accepted under certain circumstances or situations as described in the following paragraphs. Even though acceptance of a gift may be permitted by one of the exceptions, it is never inappropriate and frequently prudent for an employee to decline a gift offered by a prohibited source or because of his official position.

The exceptions are:

1. Gifts of $20 or less. An employee may accept unsolicited gifts having a market value of $20 or less per occasion, provided that the value of gifts from any one person shall not exceed $50 in a calendar year.

2. Gifts based on personal relationships. This exception allows an employee to accept a gift given under circumstances which make it clear that the gift is motivated by a family relationship or personal friendship rather than the position of the employee. Relevant factors in making such a determination include the history of the relationship and whether the family member or friend personally pays for the gift.

3. Commercial discounts and similar benefits which are available to all Government employees. This exception may include discounts and reduced organization membership fees.

4. Certain awards and honorary degrees. An employee may accept gifts, other than cash or an investment interest, with an aggregate market value of $200 or less if such gifts are a bona fide award or incident to a bona fide award that is given for meritorious public service or achievement by a person who does not have any interests that may be substantially affected by the performance or nonperformance of the employee's official duties. Exception to this $200 limit may be granted upon review of Customs DAEO.

5. Gifts from outside business activities of employees and their spouses when it is clear that such benefits have not been offered or enhanced because of the employee's official position. This also includes travel and entertainment received in connection with bona fide employment discussions for an employee who is

seeking new employment, as long as the prospective employer does not have interests that could be affected by the performance or nonperformance of the employees official duties, unless the employee has first complied with certain disqualification requirements.

6. Certain gifts from political organizations. This applies only to employees who are exempt under 5 USC 7324(d) from the Hatch Act prohibitions against active participation in political management or political campaigns.

7. Free attendance and food when employee is assigned to participate as a speaker or panel participant or otherwise to present information on behalf of the Customs Service or to appear at other widely attended gatherings that will further the Customs Service's programs or operations.

Limitations on the Use of Exceptions:

1. An employee may not use any of the exceptions to solicit or coerce the offering of a gift.

2. An employee may not accept gifts in return for being influenced in the performance of an official act.

3. An employee may not accept gifts from the same or different sources, so frequently as to appear to be using public office for private gain.

4. Additional restrictions placed on Procurement Official (Federal Acquisition Regulation, 48 CFR 3.104).

Proper Disposition of Prohibited Gifts

An employee who receives a gift that cannot be accepted may:

1. Return the item to the donor or pay the donor its market value.

2. When it is not practical to return an item because it is perishable, the item may at the discretion of the employee's supervisor or the DAEO, be given to an appropriate charity, shared within the recipients's office, or destroyed.

3. For any entertainment, favor, service, benefit or other intangible, reimburse the donor the market value. Subsequent reciprocation by the employee does not constitute reimbursement.

The Customs Service may authorize disposition or return of the gifts at Government expense. Employees may use penalty mail to forward reimbursements required or permitted under these guidelines.

An employee who, on his own initiative, promptly complies with the requirements of these guidelines will not be deemed to have improperly accepted an unsolicited gift. An employee who promptly consults with the DAEO to determine whether acceptance of an unsolicited gift is proper and who, upon the advice of the ethics official, returns the gift or otherwise disposes of the gift in accordance with these guidelines, will be considered to have complied with the requirements on his own initiative.

GIFTS BETWEEN EMPLOYEES:

GIFTS TO SUPERIORS:

In general, an employee is prohibited from giving, donating to, or soliciting contributions for, a gift to an official superior. Specifically, an employee may not:

1. Directly or indirectly, give a gift to or make a donation toward a gift for an official superior; or
2. Solicit a contribution from another employee for a gift to either his own or the other employee's official superior.

GIFTS FROM EMPLOYEES RECEIVING LESS PAY:

An employee may not, directly or indirectly, accept a gift from an employee receiving less pay than himself unless:

1. The two employees are not in a subordinate-official superior relationship; and
2. There is a personal relationship between the two employees that would justify the gift.

EXCEPTIONS TO THE GENERAL RULE:

On an occasional basis, including those occasions in which gifts are traditionally given, the following may be given to an official superior or accepted from a subordinate or other employee receiving less pay:

1. Items, other than cash, not to exceed $10 fair market value per occasion;
2. Items such as shared food and refreshments among several employees;
3. Normal personal hospitality provided at a residence provided by the employee to personal friends;
4. "Host" or "hostess" gifts;
5. Leave donated to other than immediate supervisor;
6. Traditional gift occasion such as marriage, illness, or the birth or adoption of a child; or
7. Occasions that terminate a subordinate-official superior relationship, such as retirement, resignation, or transfer.

Exceptions to Voluntary Solicitations and Contributions of Nominal Amounts from Fellow Employees for a Gift to an Official Superior

Under the following circumstances, an employee may solicit voluntary contributions of nominal amounts from fellow employees for an appropriate gift to an official superior and an employee may make a voluntary contribution of a nominal amount to an appropriate gift to an official superior:

1. On a special, infrequent occasion such as marriage, illness, or the birth or adoption of a child or on occasions that terminate a subordinate-official superior relationship, such as retirement, resignation, or transfer; or

2. On an occasional basis, for items such as food and refreshments to be shared in the office among several employees.

CONFLICTING FINANCIAL INTERESTS

A conflicting financial interest exists when an employee is taking official action in a matter in which that action has a direct or predictable effect on the employee's real or associated financial interests.

GENERAL RULE

1. The employee is prohibited from acquiring or holding conflicting interests.

2. Employees doing so may be required to sell or otherwise divest their disqualifying financial interests.

3. This prohibition may also apply to the employee's spouse and minor children.

IMPARTIALITY IN PERFORMING OFFICIAL DUTIES

The employee must ensure that he takes appropriate steps to avoid loss of impartiality, or the appearance of loss of impartiality in the performance of official duties. Specifically, an employee is prohibited by criminal statute (18 USC 208(a)), from participating personally and substantially in an official capacity in any particular matter in which, to his knowledge, he, his spouse, general partner or minor child has a financial interest, if the particular matter will have a direct and predictable effect on the interest.

GENERAL RULE

1. Certain conflicting relationships will preclude employee from acting on the particular official matter.

2. This prohibition may extend to "appearance" situations.

3. The employee is responsible for bringing the potential conflict to his superior's attention.

4. In situations in which the employee realizes that there may be a conflict, he should seek the advice of his supervisor and/or the DAEO.

SEEKING OTHER EMPLOYMENT

An employee seeking employment with an employer who may be affected by the performance or nonperformance of the employee's official duties must disqualify himself from participating in the duties related to the prospective employer.

GENERAL RULE

1. Employees must be disqualified from performing official duties if seeking employment or having another arrangement concerning prospective employment, and

2. The employee's present duties would affect the interests of the prospective employer.

3. Disqualification requirements apply to prospective employment as well as *CONCURRENT* outside employment.

4. Employee must obtain written approval (CF-3031) to have ANY concurrent outside employment, and this approval must be reviewed annually.

MISUSE OF POSITION

Employees are cautioned that they must properly use official time, information and authority.

GENERAL RULE

1. An employee shall not use his public office for his own private gain, for the endorsement of any product, service or enterprise, or for the private gain of friends, relatives, or persons with whom the employee is affiliated in a nongovernmental capacity, including nonprofit organizations of which the employee is an officer or member, and persons with whom the employee has or seeks employment or business relations.

2. An employee shall not engage in a financial transaction using nonpublic information, nor allow the improper use of nonpublic information to further his own private interest or that of another, whether through advice or recommendation, or by knowing unauthorized disclosure.

3. An employee has a duty to protect and conserve Government property and shall not use such property, or allow its use, for other than authorized purposes.

4. Unless authorized, an employee shall use official time in an honest effort to perform official duties. This applies to the employees own time as well as that of subordinates.

OUTSIDE ACTIVITIES:

In addition to the principles and standards set forth in the other subparts of 5 CFR 2635, employees are cautioned that they must comply with all laws and regulations relating to:

1. Outside employment,

2. Outside activities and

3. Personal financial obligations

These laws and regulations apply to uncompensated as well as to compensated outside activities. As a general rule, an employee who wishes to engage in outside employment or other outside activities must comply with all relevant provisions, including:

1. Prohibition on outside employment or activity that conflicts with employees official duties. Outside employment must be approved.

2. An employee may not serve other than on behalf of the United States, as an expert witness, with or without compensation, in any proceeding before a court or agency of the United States in which the United States is a party or has a direct or substantial interest, without the approval of Customs.

3. An employee may not receive compensation from any source other than the government for *teaching, speaking, or writing* that relates to the employee's official duties, unless

   a. It is the regularly established curriculum of:

      i. an established institute of higher education,

      ii. an elementary school,

      iii. a secondary school, or

   b. a program of educaiton [*sic*] or training sponsored and funded by the Federal government or by a State or local government which is not offered by 3.a.i., ii., or iii., above.

CAUTION: *ANY* outside employment must be approved.

4. An employee must be aware of limitations on use of his/her official position for fundraising activities. Employees are encouraged to seek advice from the DAEO.

5. An employee must satisfy in good faith their obligations as citizens, including all just financial obligations, especially those such as Federal, State or local taxes that are imposed by law.

SUMMARY OF 5 CFR 3101

GENERAL PROVISIONS:

In concurrence with the Office of Government Ethics, the Department of the Treasury amended Title 5 of the Code of Federal Regulations by adding a new chapter XXI, consisting of part 3101, which supplements the Standards of Ethical Conduct of Employees of the Executive Branch contained in 5 CFR part 2635.

In addition to Sections 3101.101 through 3101.104, Section 3101.110 establishes additional rules which apply specifically to United States Customs Service (USCS) employees. These additional rules provide that:

1. No employee of the United States Customs Service shall work for a customs broker, international carrier, bonded warehouse, foreign trade zone, cartman, law firm or importation department of a business, nor be employed in any private capacity related to the importation or exportation of merchandise.

2. If the spouse of a USCS employee, or other relative who is dependent on or resides with a USCS employee, is employed in a position that the employee would be prohibited from occupying by paragraph 1 of this section, the employee shall file a report of family member employment with his or her supervisor. Also, the employee shall be disqualified from participation in any matter involving the relative or the relative's employer unless an agency designee, with the advice and legal clearance of the DAEO or Office of Chief Counsel, authorized the employee to participate in the matter.

SUMMARY OF USCS PPM 51735
CONDUCT AND EMPLOYEE RESPONSIBILITIES

BACKGROUND

1. Established standards and rules for Customs employees
2. Applies to all Customs employees
3. Predecessor of 5 CFR 2635
4. Certain provisions still apply

PURPOSE

1. Assist in development of responsible conduct
2. Assist supervisors in recognizing and correcting employee misconduct
3. Make fair notice to all employees of duty to avoid misconduct
4. Provide basis for appropriate remedial action

PROVISIONS

Employees shall comply with the following:

1. Will not interfere with the rights of others
2. Shall not participate, authorize, or permit discrimination based on race, age, gender, national origin, color, religion, marital status, political preference, or physical handicap.
3. Perform duties timely, correctly, and without disrupting the performance of others
4. Strictly observe duty hours and leave procedures
5. Will be courteous and business-like
6, Will not give preferential treatment other than as authorized
7. Shall promptly report to superior any arrest, detention, conviction, and disposition for Federal, State, or local violation (Exception: minor traffic infractions)
8. Shall promptly report to superiors any legal action against you resulting from your official actions

9. Shall promptly report to superiors any knowledge of violations of laws enforced by Customs or others by employees and nonemployees

10. Shall promptly report certain integrity breaches directly to Office of Internal Affairs

11. Will become familiar with provisions contained in Customs Regulations, Part 103, concerning the publication, release, or disclosure of information to the public

12. Will comply with all applicable laws and regulations pertaining to the use, processing and storage of classified and/or sensitive information

13. Will account for, conserve, protect, or dispose of any money, property or other thing of value received by them, or coming into their possession, control or custody, or to which they have access, in accordance with established regulations and procedures

14. Will not use, or authorize the use of any Government owned or leased property, or other thing of value, for other than official purposes.

15. Will not use any badge or credential to exert influence, or obtain directly or indirectly, any privilege, favor, preferred treatment, or reward, for themselves or others, or to improperly enhance their own prestige

16. Will not transport any person in a Government owned or leased vehicle, aircraft or vessel unless that person's presence is deemed necessary to the successful completion of an official assignment or it would otherwise promote the efficiency of the Customs Service.

17. Will return all Government owned or leased property issued to them for use in carrying out their official duties upon separation, transfer or reassignment, or on demand from proper authority

18. Will carry only authorized weapons on duty, and will not unduly expose or display same

19. Will be neat, clean, and professional in appearance and dress while performing official duties

20. Will not participate in any gambling activity while on Government property. Includes sports pools, dollar poker, etc.

New Zealand Paper

NEW ZEALAND CUSTOMS SERVICE
CLIENT SERVICE INITIATIVES

INTRODUCTION

The current challenge for most customs services today is to develop new strategies for managing a continuing growth in the volume and speed of international trade, with a fixed or decreasing level of resources. We are also required to deliver services in an environment in which our responsibilities are wide in scope, and increasingly complex. This includes acting as an effective facilitator of international trade and striving to meet the service expectations of our clients, along with our traditional enforcement role.

For the New Zealand Customs Service in the past year, volume increases in goods and passenger movements continued. Import entries processed showed 6.5% growth over the previous year; 2.7 million travelers arrived by air (7.9% over 1995/96) and 2.7 million travelers exited the country (7.5% over the same period last year). The number of arriving aircraft and departing aircraft increased by 13.2% and 16.6% respectively. Since 1992, there has been a 100% increase in the volume of consignments crossing the border, a 49% increase in international passenger movements, and a 6% decrease in funding.

New Zealand Customs has put in place a comprehensive modernisation programme which is improving our ability to deliver quality client service. This has involved identifying the needs and expectations of our clients in order to establish achievable standards of service. This has also involved the development of processes which make it possible for us to measure our performance against these standards using both internal measurement and feedback from clients.

Research shows that our clients value:

• Timely and efficient service delivered at the point of need
• Ease of access to that service and a higher level of availability of staff
• Friendly, knowledgeable staff
• Getting it "right first time"
• Quick resolution of issues
• Simple and efficient procedures

In 1994, the New Zealand Customs Service commissioned a market research company to annually provide an independent assessment of our service delivery. The overall objectives were to assess and analyse current levels of customer service satisfaction amongst New Zealand Customs' key customer groups; and the impact of employees attitudes on customer service. This has allowed us to gain an in depth understanding of the needs of our clients, and because these measurements are conducted annually, we have been able to use the initial results as a benchmark to track improvements in our clients' degree of satisfaction with our level of client service delivery.

The following figures illustrate some examples of the improvements we have achieved in our client service ratings:

SERVICE ATTRIBUTES	1994	1996
Innovative	53%	77%
Adaptable	57%	80%
Accessible	76%	87%
Forward thinking	54%	75%
Provide good service	84%	95%
Approachable and friendly	91%	96%

Our Strategic Plan was our means of putting a focus upon and extending our Client Service programme. In particular, the adoption of a more pro-active approach to meeting our clients' needs. Our Client Service Programme consists of a range of strategic initiatives including revision of our legislation, changes to the way we work and new systems for our clients, liaison with industry, and development of our staff.

LEGISLATION

New Zealand Customs was experiencing an increasing level of difficulty in applying the Customs Act of 1966 to provide for the expectations of the government, while meeting and matching the facilitation needs of the commercial community with those of principal departments that require customs to exercise controls over goods and persons at the border.

This legislation was proving to be overly prescriptive and rigid in structure, and did not allow us to react as quickly or flexibly as modern day business practice requires. To overcome such impediments we decided to design a completely new Act.

Our new Customs and Excise Act, which was introduced in 1996, is the most comprehensive revision of our customs law this century and has been designed to meet the needs of our clients (individuals, commerce, and the government) for the foreseeable future.

Under the new act, the name of our administration changed to the "New Zealand Customs Service". Like the Korea Customs Service, the inclusion of the word "Service" is very significant as it reflects the deliberate and ongoing change in the orientation of our organisation from a control to a service philosophy. The reaction by our clients to the Act has been extremely positive since its introduction a year ago.

Electronic access for staff to the Customs and Excise Act, Regulations and operational policy and procedures has been established through a new computer based system of "electronic documentation." Officers throughout the country have on-line read and print access through a computer to an electronic documentation system that contains:

- What's new in Customs (a daily news/advice document)
- The Act and Regulations
- Explanatory notes to both the Act and the Regulations
- policy for all departmental functions, including operational and other policy areas

The new act has provided the base for all our modernisation initiatives. It has enabled more innovation than the previous statute and this was put to good use in the design of new procedures and processes that enable us to enhance our service delivery. Our aim is to be fair and consistent but with the flexibility required to meet the needs of our clients. We are still in control of the border but we now specifically endeavour to exercise our functions in ways which will not inconvenience the honest importer or exporter or add unnecessarily to the costs they face.

The scope of the new act has been limited to those matters which must be included. To the greatest extent possible, material of an administrative or management nature has been dealt with in ways other than inclusion in the statute (i.e., regulations or administrative directions). In line with the direction set in our Strategic Plan the act deliberately removes unnecessary prescription and introduces administrative flexibility.

A good example of this is in the area of excise licensees. The new legislation allows for periodic entries for smaller excise licensees which means such licensees do not have to bear the cost of preparing monthly accounts for customs use. Now they need to provide only one return a year for everything they manufacture. Also, under the previous Act all licensees had to make their excise payments by the twenty-first day of every month. Deadlines for making excise payments are now established under regulations instead of being set down in our new act. This means the times that payments must be made can be extended out to the end of the month, which provides significant cash flow advantages for excise licensees.

As we now have greater administrative flexibility we have made our decision making more transparent, and created access for our clients to a low cost and independent appeal structure (the Customs Appeal Authorities) to challenge our decisions.

The introduction of the new act symbolises the new way we want to work in the New Zealand Customs Service. Our new client focus recognises that customs exists to provide a service and our aim is to be fair and consistent but with the flexibility required to meet the needs of our clients.

CHANGING THE WAY WE WORK

The initiatives introduced under our Customs Modernisation Project, which we named CusMod, are a major aspect of our new strategic direction. CusMod consisted of four subprojects:

- Intelligence
- Client Service
- Goods and Revenue
- Passenger Processing

The CusMod project commenced in late 1995, and was implemented starting in 1996 using a phased approach over two years to minimize disruption to clients and to take account of the ability of the organisation to adjust to change. By incrementally approaching the change customs was able to deliver early benefits and place greater focus on client liaison and services.

By replacing existing paper based and computer systems with more advanced electronic alternatives customs is now able to provide clients with better, faster tools and integrated information systems.

The key features of the new business processes for client service include:

- A single group which handles all general telephone enquiries with the ability to refer to specialised work areas if required
- A single integrated facility for the processing of all types of goods
- Emphasis on liaising with those clients who need further assistance
- empowerment of front line staff through improved access to high quality information

Under our new intelligence system, Import entries and passenger movements are electronically compared with the intelligence database to identify people and other transactions of interest. Intelligence assessments and alerts ensure that on a nationwide basis New Zealand Customs is targeting the areas of greatest risk. This risk is established at a national level in accordance with government priorities. Therefore Intelligence contributes to our ability to provide improved client service through the minimum intervention to legitimate trade and travel.

National Call Centre

A centralised national call centre was introduced in 1996 to provide accurate, consistent advice to clients who contact customs through a toll-free phone number. An on-line Business Support Tool which has access to information such as prohibitions, exchange rates, duty rates, and publications, provides Call Centre staff with ready access to general information, allowing them to provide immediate answers to the majority of client enquiries.

Clients get a complete answer with one call and if the question cannot be answered by Call Centre personnel, the caller is transferred to the appropriate specialist work area. Currently staff answer 90% of calls without needing to transfer. Calls received outside normal working hours are forwarded to a cellphone carried by a Client Service officer to provide a twenty-four-hour service.

The Call Centre gives clients better quality service because its computer-based information system can be updated immediately to ensure the information customs provides is always consistent, current and accurate, and its specialised staff have been trained to perform to a high standard in all aspects of enquiry handling and client focus.

The Business Support Tool is also available to staff at enquiry counters in all our district offices nationwide so that clients calling in personally have access to the same quality information.

Client service initiatives have resulted in improved accessibility for clients to New Zealand Customs and improved client communication. The consistency of advice provided to clients on a national basis and the accuracy and completeness of this information result in a reduction in the time spent by our clients in seeking assistance and a decrease in the likelihood of error when they complete entry requirements. This results in reduced compliance costs for business and better educated clients who are able to comply more easily and are happier to do so because they clearly understand requirements.

Client service initiatives have also created a better utilisation of resources. The reduced demand on operations staff through the removal of interruptions caused by answering client enquiries has allowed a better focus on core business in specialized technical areas leading to improved efficiency and processing times. Identification of growth industries to determine the future growth of our client base has enabled us to identify where our resources should best be targeted.

Our New Approach

The new goods management processes which have been developed focus on processing as much information as possible electronically, identifying transactions of interest automatically through the use of intelligence processes, scheduling Inspections and Audit to better utilise staff and resources, and electronically filing information reports for intelligence use.

Delivering information electronically reduces the staff required by our clients to prepare and deliver paper information, provides consistency in the processing of all entry types, and enables the majority of entries to be cleared through customs within minutes.

This produces gains in efficiency and effectiveness, greater accuracy and timeliness for trade data and reduced compliance costs. The result is clients who are motivated to comply to achieve the benefits of predictable clearance times that assist with Just in Time management.

Our Regional Collectors (Northern, Central and Southern) are proactively developing a stronger focus on client liaison and development of continuous improvement processes which will ensure a new approach to researching and responding to client needs. Customs will widely broadcast new initiatives developed to meet predicted and actual client concerns, and the client liaison role undertaken by Customs Key Account managers has been extended to build in a facility where contact with clients will be triggered by a particular event, action or need.

LIAISON WITH CLIENT GROUPS

The creation, earlier this year, of a Joint Industry Consulting Group, is part of the New Zealand Customs Service's strategy to build a liaison with industry. The establishment of the group resulted from a series of interviews conducted with key industry contacts to determine their level of understanding of CusMod, and to assess whether they could identify the tangible benefits that the modernisation project would provide to them. The interviews indicated that there was a high degree of satisfaction with the initiatives that were being developed under the project, and a sound basis for the improvement of business relationships and communication with industry groups through establishing strategic level dialogue between customs and industry.

The Joint Industry Consulting Group is providing the impetus for the next phase of continuous improvements to our client service delivery. Six industry groups were asked to nominate a representative who understood their business and who could contribute to discussions across the full spectrum of customs interaction with industry. The groups which are represented are: Customs Brokers and Freight Forwarders; Airlines; Importers; Exporters; Air Express Interests; and Port companies. The New Zealand Customs Service is represented by the Comptroller of Customs and a small group of senior staff.

Key tasks for the joint industry consulting group include the immediate transfer of the benefits of customs modernisation to industry groups, and the identification of statutory and regulatory barriers associated with customs activity, the removal or modification of which could enhance the activities of these industries.

DEVELOPING OUR PEOPLE

Now that the systems part of our modernisation program is in place, our objective is to ensure an understanding of, and commitment to, client service is shared throughout the organization, is consistent, and can be demonstrated externally in what customs does and how it does it.

New Zealand Customs' modernisation is important, not only about replacing or upgrading technology and processes, but also about developing and taking care our people so that we can get the maximum benefit from the new technology and processes. Successful modernisation requires the commitment of staff and different behaviors and competencies to maximize the benefits of the new systems and processes. We are therefore placing a great deal of emphasis on human resource initiatives.

Our human resources strategy will ensure that these new behaviors are fully incorporated into our new structure by developing processes that measure client servicing and allow the adoption by staff of client service values to be recognized and rewarded appropriately. This flows into role descriptions, performance measures, performance management systems, recognition, and rewards and remuneration strategies.

CONCLUSION

In order to achieve excellence in an increasingly competitive environment, the New Zealand Customs Service chooses to compete on the basis of Superior Quality of Service Delivery, where "Quality" is defined as delivering a level of service which meets or exceeds our client's expectations.

According to the results of our latest Client Satisfaction Survey, 91% of our clients are satisfied with the service they personally receive from us. This rating has been consistent over the last three years:

* 65% think that the service we provide has improved over the last two years
* 76% predict further improvements in our performance in the future

Now that our modernisation initiatives have transformed the business processes of the whole organization, our new human resources strategy will ensure that client service, and a commitment to and understanding of our "Service Vision" are an important, credible and recognised success criteria. The measurement processes we have developed to determine our clients' satisfaction with the service we provide will allow us to continually assess and improve our performance.

Washington Declaration

DECLARATION OF THE CUSTOMS CO-OPERATION COUNCIL CONCERNING HARMONIZATION/COMPUTERIZATION OF CUSTOMS PROCEDURES AND A STRATEGY FOR THE 21ST CENTURY
(Washington Declaration)
(July 1989)

NOTING that progress has been made towards achievement of international uniformity in the classification of goods (the Harmonized System), in Customs valuation (the GATT Valuation Code), in Customs procedures (Kyoto Convention) and in enforcement (Nairobi Convention),

RECOGNIZING that one of the principal objectives of the CCC is to secure the highest degree of harmony and uniformity in Customs systems,

REALIZING that the Ottawa Declaration provides for standardization, simplification and harmonization of Customs processes, procedures and documents,

RECOGNIZING that the major members of the international trade community are committed to replacing paper with electronic information management and that Customs administrations have to follows suit,

NOTING the important role of Customs administrations in facilitating, monitoring, reporting on, and controlling the movement of world trade,

REALIZING that by the year 2000 Customs administrations which still rely on paper records might be able to maintain their role in world trade only with increasing difficulties and risks,

ACKNOWLEDGING that the CCC is already working on many different areas that relate to the request for more standardization and automation,

FURTHER acknowledging that Customs administrations vary in their ability to adapt to modern data management technologies, and that more needs to be done to ensure that Customs administrations keep up with advancing trade volume and technology,

THE CUSTOMS CO-OPERATION COUNCIL,

DECLARES that the Council should immediately undertake a comprehensive, structured, coordinated initiative in the area of simplification, standardization and harmonization of Customs procedures,

DECLARES further, insofar as automation is concerned, that the Council should,

(1) evaluate, and keep Members informed of, the impact of new developments,

(2) provide advice and guidance and launch special programmes for those Members still dependent on paper records to assist them in streamlining current procedures, in adopting progressively automated techniques and in resolving difficulties (e.g. with electronic signatures and other legal issues),

(3) seek access for Members to additional resources to implement automation and EDI by co-operating closely with other governmental and non-governmental international organizations,

(4) urge Members now using automation to move towards adoption of full electronic data interchange, based on modular hardware that allows for efficient updating of technology,

(5) continue to take the lead, in close co-operation with the UN Economic Commission for Europe, in promoting and enlarging EDI FACT as a standard for the electronic interchange of Customs information among its Members, international organizations and other participants in international trade,

(6) identify standard Customs requirements for EDI in all international fora,

(7) stress the importance of working closely with commerce and transport organizations at the national and international level in promoting EDI initiatives,

(8) help to develop and promote affordable, routine electronic exchanges between and among traders and Customs organizations,

(9) identify Members' training needs in automation and seek to arrange for this training with the assistance, where necessary, of Member administrations and other international organizations, and

(10) assist Members in enhancing their enforcement efforts by employing EDI.

DECIDES that, given the number, complexity and variety of Customs procedures in existence worldwide, the development of guidelines or harmonized procedural frameworks should be pursued in addition to existing standards,

DIRECTS that, having regard to the resources available and the priorities set out in the Plan for the '90's,

1. the Permanent Technical Committee should undertake a new task of standardization and go beyond the Kyoto Convention in this area, while building on the foundations laid in that Convention, and

2. the ADP Sub-Committee should develop concrete work-plans for the tasks in automation described above,

INSTRUCTS the Secretary General to take such further steps as may be necessary to implement this Declaration.

Ottawa Declaration

DECLARATION OF THE COUNCIL
FOR MEETING THE CHALLENGES OF THE YEAR 2000
(Ottawa Declaration)
(June 1987)

THE CUSTOMS CO-OPERATION COUNCIL,

NOTING that the Convention establishing a Customs Co-operation Council gave as its purpose:

"to secure the highest degree of harmony and uniformity in Customs systems and especially to study the problems inherent in the development and improvement of Customs technique and Customs legislation . . .",

"to promote co-operation between governments in these matters, bearing in mind the economic and technical factors involved",

NOTING that the Council's Plan for the 1980's has guided the Council's work in an organized and productive fashion,

HAVING REGARD to the Conventions and Declarations previously adopted by the Council, specifically the Seoul and the Brussels Declarations,

RECOGNIZING that the period leading up to the year 2000 will present a variety of challenges to Customs administrations world-wide and will require concerted and co-ordinated efforts to keep pace with the environmental changes which will precipitate these challenges, including:

—growing international trade and interchange, and global interdependence,

—growth in world population; increasing concern for the global environment,

—substantial increase in international travel, illicit drug traffic, prohibited goods and commercial fraud,

—technological advances in communications, transportation and detection techniques,

RECOGNIZING that such developments will have an increasing impact on Customs administrations and will bring into question the appropriateness of existing Customs operations and procedures,

CONSIDERS that the CCC should continue:

—promoting the adoption of the Harmonized System, the GATT Valuation Code and the Kyoto Convention as standard bases for tariff classification, valuation and Customs procedures in modern trade,

—ensuring uniform application of the Harmonized System and Valuation Systems,

—promoting further development of standard documentation and uniform Customs procedures to simplify Customs processes and remove barriers to international trade, and

—developing improved methods of control and enforcement and generating co-operation among Members to ensure that Customs services are able to respond to the serious problems of narcotic traffic and commercial fraud facing them in the next decade.

CONSIDERS that it is necessary to review and confirm the Council objectives as the basis for the Plan for the 1990's which will reflect Member's needs in a modern Customs environment, and considering that needs will have to be established in a period of financial restraint,

DECLARES:

—that it will endorse the development of a planning perspective which takes account of changing world conditions during the next decade and will prepare Customs administrations for the foreseeable challenges of the year 2000;

—that the primary objectives of the Council for the 1990's will be:

I.   to encourage harmonization and simplification of Customs processes and to promote co-operation among Customs administrations by:

(A) in respect of the Harmonized System, promoting the widest application of the System for Customs tariffs, for production, trade and transport statistics, for freight tariffs and for commercial commodity description and coding systems through:

—updating regularly the system to reflect changes in technology and in patterns of international trade so that it continues to be a relevant document for purposes of modern trade,

—securing uniformity in the interpretation and application of the System by preparing Explanatory Notes, Classification Opinions, or other advice and recommendations, and collecting and circulating information concerning the application of the System,

—developing a data base for the aforesaid purposes, including a system for collection and dissemination of national classification decisions of interest to Members, thus enabling the CCC to act as a clearing house on classification matters,

(B) promoting the widest adoption and implementation of the GATT Valuation Code by providing technical assistance and advice to Members while ensuring uniform application of the Brussels Definition of Value by those countries still applying it, and

—developing a data base and a system for the collection and dissemination of national value decisions which will permit the CCC to act as a clearing house on value matters,

(C) developing and promoting standard Customs documents for multiple Customs procedures and standardized data systems permitting automated exchange of data,

(D) studying modern Customs processes, developing standardized and simplified Customs procedures and intensifying promotion of the Kyoto Convention and other Council instruments which advocate such processes and procedures,

(E) actively identifying new techniques and disseminating information about them among Members, with practical implementation measures,

II. to develop improved control and enforcement capabilities by:

(A) working in collaboration with Members and interested organizations in developing ADP techniques and systems of relevance to the Customs,

(B) studying new Customs control methods to ensure adequacy of enforcement while simplifying and speeding up Customs processes,

(C) promoting greater co-operation in the enforcement area by developing programmes and strategies to fully implement the Brussels Declaration through:

—intensifying adoption of the Nairobi Convention and Council instruments which provide for mutual assistance and co-operation,

—maximizing exchange of information and intelligence by the most timely and efficient means,

—increasing co-operation and exchange of information through computer systems with other enforcement agencies, both nationally and internationally,

III. to improve the human resources, the organization and management of Customs administrations by:

(A) promoting regional programmes and regional initiatives in training of Customs officers and officer exchange programmes,

(B) providing a forum for management-level discussions on topical Customs questions,

(C) developing programmes and strategies for implementing the Seoul Declaration through the development of model training programmes and the provision of expert assistance, particularly in relation to the Harmonized System and the GAU Valuation Code,

AND re-emphasizing that International Customs Day, January 26, will be an occasion for all Members to promote the image of Customs services and to make their objectives and role better known to users and the general public,

DIRECTS THE SECRETARY GENERAL to take such steps as may be necessary to implement this Declaration.

△ △ △

Selected Bibliography

Bernstein, Peter L. *Against the Gods: The Remarkable Story of Risk*. New York: John Wiley & Sons, 1996.

Brandenburger, Adam M., and Barry J. Nalebuff. *Co-opetition*. New York: Doubleday, 1996.

Davis, Stan. *Future Perfect*. Reading, Mass.: Addison-Wesley, 1996.

Goldstein, Herman. *Problem-Oriented Policing*. New York: McGraw Hill, 1990.

Hamel, Gary, and C. K. Prehalad. *Competing for the Future*. Boston: Harvard Business School Press, 1994.

Harrington, H. James. *Business Process Improvement*. New York: McGraw Hill, 1991.

Kanter, Rosabeth. *World Class: Thriving Locally in a Global Economy*. New York: Simon & Schuster, 1995.

Low, Patrick. *Preshipment Inspection Services*. Washington, D.C.: World Bank Discussion Papers, 1995.

Mintzberg, Henry. "Managing Government, Governing Management." *Harvard Business Review*, May–June 1996.

Nohria, Nitin, and James D. Berkely. "What Ever Happened to the Take-Charge Manager?" *Harvard Business Review*, January–February 1994.

Nonaka, Ikujiro, and Hirotaka Takeuchi. *The Knowledge-Creating Company*. New York: Oxford University Press, 1995.

Quinn, James Brian. *Intelligent Enterprise*. New York: Free Press, 1992.

Smith, Adam. *An Inquiry into the Nature and Causes of the Wealth of Nations*. Chicago: University of Chicago Press, 1976.

Sparrow, Malcolm K. *Imposing Duties: Government's Changing Approach to Compliance*. Westport, Conn.: Praeger, 1994.

Stares, Paul B. *Global Habit: The Drug Problem in a Borderless World*. Washington, D.C.: The Brookings Institution, 1996.

Walker, Donald E. *Never Try to Teach a Pig to Sing*. San Diego: Lathrop Press, 1996.

World Bank. *Global Economic Prospects in the Developing World*. Washington, D.C.: World Bank Discussion Papers, 1995.

Index

△ △ △

ABOUT THE AUTHOR

MICHAEL H. LANE is currently President of Global Customs Advisors. He is also the International Customs Advisor to the U.S. Council for International Business. Mr. Lane has served as Deputy Commissioner of U.S. Customs, and Deputy Assistant Secretary of the Department of Treasury.